MW00593570

MORE HOMICIDAL HUMOR

....

THE KNIFE AND GUN CLUB

SGT. BRIAN FOSTER

As it was.

Black Dog Swamp Publishing Co.
Rosharon, Texs

Black Dog Swamp Publishing Co.
Rosharon, TX 77583
www.homicidalhumor.com

Publisher's Note: This is a work of fiction. Names, characters,
places, and incidents are a product of the author's imagination.
Locales and public names are sometimes used for atmospheric
purposes. Any resemblance to actual people, living or dead, or
to businesses, companies, events, institutions, or locales is
completely coincidental.

Book Layout ©2013 BookDesignTemplates.com

More Homicidal Humor/Brian Foster. – 2nd ed.
ISBN 978-0-9837073-1-8

Contents

Author Name

Acknowledgement and Thanks

I would like to take a moment to acknowledge a few people for their help and assistance. First I thank my wife and son for both putting up with and encouraging me while I compiled and spun these stories from my stagnant and eclectic mind. Second, I would like to thank my friends Chris and Virginia who felt sorry for a computer illiterate. Without their help neither of my books would ever have ever come to pass. I may never become a bestselling author, but it will not be because I didn't have the best support staff on the planet.

DISCLAIMER

Once again I must claim that all of the information contained in this book (as in my previous one) is only fictional material. Any resemblance to persons living, dead or simply brain dead is strictly a coincidence. The first story in this book, as well as the three others about the deaths of Dirty Red, Felton Coleman, and Poor Willie are true. The names of all persons except Horace "Bully" Paul have been changed. The rather colorful statements found in the chapter entitled Quotes from the Uncouth may have been spoken in my presence and collected by me when they occurred. There again, for the sake of liability, they may not have.

Back when I began policing I was taught that idiots were put on this earth to entertain those of us who had to deal with them. I would like to now officially thank the scores of idiots I have dealt with for all of the source material they provided. I would also like to thank the officers who shared their war stories with me. I am not able to recall who told me what story, or when or where I was when they were told to me. I was never present at any of the events that appear in this book. If I had been I would never admit to it anyway.

If some of you are offended by the stories in this book—too bad. Nobody really likes you anyway. What's more, I'm sure your mother dressed you funny when you were a child. Her actions surely caused you to become the social outcast you are today. Now have a good read, my friend.

ONE

BULLY PAUL

Horace Paul was his given name, but since childhood he had been known by the name of Bully. In the old west he would have been known as a bad man. It is not that he was evil or a criminal, but he was simply a bad man to cross or to mess with. He was not a monster in stature, but was as strong as two mules and not afraid to back up what he had to say. There again, he was also not a psalm singer nor did the milk of human kindness ever really bubble up from his inner soul so that you could see it. In many ways, however, he was the actual character that John Wayne tried to portray in old westerns. Bully Paul lived that life for five and one half decades and went out in a stand-up gunfight. His last battle was an up-close-and-personal exchange of gunfire where both he and his killer died. It should also be noted he died protecting another person. This man would have told you that going out the way he did beat the hell out of dying of natural causes while lying in some hospital bed with a tube up your nose.

Bully's dad (for whom he was named) ran beer joints in southeast Houston. His mother was a deputy sheriff and worked in the Harris County Jail. From the time he was fourteen or fifteen his father used him as a bouncer in his working class beer joint. Horace Paul (the senior) usually kept a single action revolver stuck in the front of his pants and he was not afraid to use it either as a club or a handgun. After high school young Paul joined the Marines and was treated to an all-expenses paid tour of South Vietnam. He earned a Purple Heart there, and after his tour of duty he returned to Houston and the beer joint business. When his dad retired Bully closed his place and took over the family icehouse/bar at the intersection of Telephone and Almeda Genoa Roads. By this point in his life the youngest of the Paul boys was a two-fisted drinking brawler running his own place in his own way. About once a month he would have to show someone just how he had earned his reputation.

Bully worked hard, drank hard, and played hard. Some mornings you could find him at the ice house sipping a beer while he was waiting for the coffee to finish perking. Consuming up to three cases of beer in a single day was not unheard of. He was known to help out a lot of people, both those that he knew and some that he did not. One area grocery owner reported seeing Bully

4

standing in a checkout line behind a woman and her son. They both were skinny and looked down and out. She had only two items she was buying, those being rice and pinto beans. Bully handed the woman two one hundred dollar bills and admonished her saying, "Woman, that kid needs more groceries and a warm jacket. Now go take care of that."

If a regular customer didn't have the money to get his car out of the shop, Bully often would stand good for the bill. He didn't charge interest, but you'd better make your payments to him, though. If you didn't he would have to hunt you down. You see, on Telephone Road you can't let a whore or a nickel-and-dime thief beat you out of money. If you let it happen then a whole slew of idiots will line up to try and rob you blind. The man in question was also known to whip somebody's ass because he'd heard that man had recently beaten his wife. That may have only been all the excuse he really needed a time or two—who knows.

Over the years running such an establishment, Bully was involved in multiple shooting situations. Some were reported to the cops while others were not. Most of the bar fights went unreported. Many in the beer joint crowd were thought to hang out there just so they might have a ring side seat to the next event. Here are a couple of highlights from some of the shootings that took place over the years.

One night there was a domino game going on at a table up against the south wall. A skinny black male walked into the joint and walked straight away up to the game. He pulled a gun from his jacket pocket and began cursing everyone and demanding money. Bully was standing behind the bar and had a clear shot at Stupid. Paul's right hand, however, was in a cast from an earlier altercation, so he was forced to shoot left-handed. The weapon of the day was a Colt government model in .38 Super caliber. As the barkeep banged away at the man (later identified posthumously as Tyrone Malone) the would-be robber was literally spinning around. What was happening was that Bully was only making peripheral hits and not any center-of-body strikes.

Stupid finally hit the floor after taking three less than solid body shots. The wounded robber was lying on the floor trying to clear his own gun which had jammed. Bully ran out from behind the bar and kicked the idiot in the head with the toe of his cowboy boot. Witnesses said the kick was delivered with such force that the wounded man's head snapped like a football coming off a kicking tee. One of Bully's rounds had gone from side-to-side completely through the jacker's mouth, coursing through his cheeks and exiting the far side of his face. An autopsy the next morning would determine that none of the dead man's gunshot wounds were fatal. The actual cause of death came about when Mrs. Paul's son kicked Stupid in the head. The blow to his temple was such that it caused considerable blunt force trauma. That kick, not the bullets, brought about the urban blight removal of one armed robbery suspect. Bully never again had any use for .38 Super caliber pistols after that experience. Thereafter he would, however, sing the praises of steel-toed boots.

The morning after this shooting (while cleaning up the bloody mess) one of Tyrone's molars was found on the bar room floor. Bully saved it and had it mounted on a plaque along with a Polaroid picture of the dead man lying on the beer joint floor. The shooting trophy still resides in the display case that runs across the back wall of the club.

Another shooting incident began after a rowdy redneck was ejected from the icehouse one summer afternoon. The man in question had a mouth on him, but he showed no desire to bait the badger, as it were. Being drunk is one thing, and being stupid is yet another. Drunk *and* stupid can, however, lead you to some serious grief. So it was on the day in question. Stupid climbed into his pickup which was parked outside the club's front overhead doors. The club's doors were open as usual. Stupid pulled a gun out and pointed it at Bully through the front windshield of his truck. Bully himself was armed as usual and proceeded to fire multiple rounds in yon redneck's windshield, punching all manner of 9mm holes into the drunk's body. Bully then ran out and jerked the shot-up drunkard from his truck. While waiting for paramedics to arrive Bully applied his first aid skills to save the life of the man who had just pointed a gun at him. He might shoot the hell out of you for pointing a gun at him, but he wouldn't let you bleed to death while you waited for an ambulance. That is, unless he really didn't like you for some reason, and as long as you were white.

Bully Paul declined on the filing of aggravated assault charges against the redneck. Besides, the redneck was facing felony charges for having a gun on licensed premises anyway. Bully's gun was tagged in the property room. The redneck lived and was prosecuted for his felony handgun case. Bully got his gun back after that case was disposed of and life went on. The cops in Houston understand that there are some folks out there that just need shooting. Besides, Bully never had a shortage of spare guns.

Unlike John Wayne, Bully liked horses. He was a trail rider at times and would party with the best of them. Bully was also a regular at barbeque cook-offs and rodeos. He also became involved with a group called Texas Equi-Search. This group puts together searches for missing children and the elderly, and helped in police searches of large areas when bodies or evidence were

8

being sought. Whenever there was a search Bully would show up with a flatbed trailer and several four-wheeler motorcycles to help out.

Horace (Bully) Paul cheated death on several occasions. He had his throat cut at the boxing matches when he was between eleven and thirteen and somehow survived. He was shot when he was in the Marine Corps while serving in Vietnam. He had been in multiple brawls and shooting situations. His liver tried to eat him alive and he proved them wrong at the VA Hospital a couple of times when they said he was going to die behind his drinking. After one of his sons died from leukemia he fell off the wagon and began drinking again.

On the day Bully died he had thrown a pool party at his house. One of his female employees attended the blowout and had too much to drink, so he drove her home. That employee, though she was married, had been involved in an affair with a customer who lived in nearby Pearland. The man in question turned out to be a nut case and he made her life miserable. Lover Boy had been banned from Paul's bar under the penalty of getting his butt kicked.

Bully dropped the drunken barmaid off at her house on Dillon Street and was backing out of the driveway as she was opening her front door. She turned and ran back to Paul's truck yelling that somebody was in the house and they had a gun. Bully was licensed to carry a concealed handgun and he was never one to sit on the fence. As usual, he chose to jump into the middle of things. He went into the house with his .45 Colt in his hand. Horace Paul Jr. immediately came under fire as he entered the front door, taking two solid hits to the body. Paul center-punched his adversary with a .45-caliber hollow-point bullet just a millisecond before he himself was shot once more.

Bully's last wound was from a bullet to the face, and that round exited the back of his head. Both men lay dead on the floor only a few feet apart. The former boyfriend had broken into the rear portion of Sweet Thing's house. He then rummaged around in the house and found his former squeeze's husband's 9mm Taurus pistol. Romeo then sat in the front room waiting for Sweet Thing to return.

Horace "Bully" Paul's funeral was attended by one hell of an unusual cross section of humanity. In attendance were uniformed cops, firemen, bikers, goat ropers, construction workers, and a whole host of Middle America. His passing was even noted on the front page of the Houston Chronicle newspaper. The man went out in a manner that he would have approved of. He was truly a legend in Southeast Houston and on Telephone Road. Many men would like to be bigger than life. Some are so only in their own minds. There are some men who are bad asses, but they tend to amount to nothing and are not revered as being real men. Those who actually achieve such a status seem not to actively seek it out. Neither can they deny just who and what they really are. Such was the case with Horace (Bully) Paul. Paul's Ice House is still located at the intersection of Telephone and Almeda Genoa Roads and is still run by members of the Paul family. Bully's United States Marine Corps flag also still hangs on the wall of the establishment. Semper Fi.

TWO

....

TO CATCH A THIEF

Jeff Adams worked the 3 p.m. to 11 p.m. shift out of the Beechnut Station. He lived in Pearland in an upper middle class neighborhood on a cul de sac. He would go back home to Hallettsville, Texas every month or two. One fall he returned home to Pearland with an iron frame that he and his father built to hold cordwood, and a pickup bed full of split oak. He set the fireplace wood rack on the side of his house but not inside his backyard fence. After the first cold snap that year, Jeff began noticing he was missing firewood, particularly on Saturday and Sunday mornings. He suspected Rajah Patel, his dot-head East Indian neighbor, was stealing his firewood but he could not prove it. Adams discussed the theft over a beer with his redneck neighbor from across the street. That neighbor was a pus-gutted individual who was quite appropriately known as Bubba. Bubba Langston worked as an installer for home and commercial security systems and he told Jeff that he would work out a system by which they might either identify or catch the thief and stop the problem all together.

One Thursday night just before another cold snap Bubba called Jeff on his cell phone. He told Jeff it was very important for him not to use any of the cord wood on his stack, and if he wanted to make a fire to come get some wood from the stack just inside Bubba's back gate. Bubba said he'd laid a trap for the thief and if anyone disturbed the wood pile it would ruin the whole program. Jeff figured Bubba had set up some sort of motion-activated detector or infrared camera system, because that was what the man did for a living in the security industry. Two nights later, Jeff came home from work at thirty minutes before midnight to find a fire department pumper truck in front of his dot-head neighbor's house. It seems that neighbor must have had a creosote buildup inside the flue of his chimney. This resulted in a minor explosion and the carpet inside that neighbor's den caught on fire.

Sunday after church, Jeff saw Bubba for the first time in a week. Bubba told him he thought Jeff's theft problems were most likely over for good and that he (Bubba) needed to retrieve one or two of the extra pieces of cordwood he had donated to the Adams' family wood source. Jeff asked the local resident redneck how he'd implemented the loss prevention program. Bubba said that he had heard somewhere that if a body drilled a big enough hole in each end of a piece of cordwood that he could drop a twenty-gauge shotgun shell inside them. Then if he whittled down a tree limb he could plug that hole and make it look untouched and quite natural. For some reason the cordwood thefts stopped immediately from the Adams house.

A good redneck friend or neighbor can at times be a definite asset, but you had better keep your homeowner's liability insurance policy paid up. You also need high dollar coverage, which maybe includes an umbrella policy with a million or so dollars of exposure and your deductible may also need to be lowered.

THREE

....

COMMENDATION DECLINED

Patrol officer Michael Kevin O'Brien was called into his sergeant's office and handed a letter of commendation from a citizen. He was told by his immediate supervisor that he needed to sign and date the document if he wanted it to appear in his personnel file.

O'Brien read it and said, "That's all a damned lie and I did nothing of the sort." His sergeant asked, "You don't want a letter of commendation in your personnel file?" O'Brien's response was "Hell no, throw it away. I refuse to sign the damned thing."

The incident that never occurred had taken place at the end of a particularly stressful shift for O'Brien. The "good" letter was addressed to Houston's Chief of Police and read as follows.

Dear Sir,

I would like to commend Officer M.K. O'Brien for showing compassion and understanding while dealing with me the other evening. I had been experiencing some family problems and responded poorly by using alcohol to excess. Officer O'Brien pulled me over near the intersection of San Filepe and Voss. I pulled into a parking lot where he interviewed me. I acknowledged that I had been drinking after experiencing some family problems. Your officer took my car keys and threw them into some nearby bushes. He told me that when I was sober enough to find my keys then I would be sober enough to drive home safely. I spent the night in my car and feel I am a better man for the experience. He could have put me in jail and cost me a lot of money and embarrassment. Instead he showed compassion for his fellow man. I would like to tell you what an asset you have in him.

John Howard Connor

FOUR

....

CLOVERLEAF

Interstate 10 runs east out of Houston towards Louisiana. It only takes about three hours to get to the Louisiana state line from downtown Houston. The area east of Houston is low-lying and the petrochemical industries have plants scattered for ninety miles east of Houston's city limits. The unincorporated area between the cities of Houston and Baytown is generally called either Cloverleaf or Sheldon. Cloverleaf has the highest rates of family violence in all of Harris County, Texas and Sheldon (also called Beaumont Place) has the highest rates of incest in the county. The inhabitants of the area are typically blue collar Anglos and Hispanics and are in some ways very unusual. There are some exceptionally beautiful women in the area, but they could be organ donors at any time because they all tend to be brain-dead. The Anglo males of the species (*north americanus redneck vulgarus*) tend toward a *four on the floor and a fifth on the seat* mentality. The area residents that like and use drugs would rather inject them than to use them otherwise. They are still working on a system by which they might mainline marijuana smoke into their veins without fatal results. Social lives tend to center around beer joints and barbeque pits. If Billy Graham were to set up a mega-church thereabouts it would get its best attendance if set up inside the locally famous Double Bayou Dance Hall and Saloon. But, I digress.

Two detectives called Lumpy and Delmar (by their coworkers) were assigned to make a DOA/floater in Greens Bayou just south of Interstate 10 one Saturday afternoon. Floaters are cases that you have to work in stages. First you attempt to identify the dead person. Then you hope the medical examiner can tell you the cause of death. Upon finding out just who the dearly departed was, then you move on to attempting to determine where and how they died. To get there you work backwards from where the dead person in question was last seen, and in whose company. The other variables you work with are animals and weather conditions.

On the Texas Gulf Coast you have mostly tropical weather with warm temperatures and high humidity. The animals that live in and around the bayous and waterways will also take a body apart in a hurry. Turtles and crabs go to work immediately on any exposed skin areas. Lips, ears, eyes and fingers go the quickest. Gar fish will bite off chunks of exposed flesh when given a chance. People are always greatly surprised that blue crabs will travel up to ninety miles upstream from the Gulf of Mexico.

Back to the scene. The body was that of a white male and he was hung up on some brush at the water's edge. It is generally never immediately known where the remains got into the water, and the body at the scene tends to be your only physical evidence when beginning your investigation. While Lumpy and Delmar were waiting on the dive team and medical examiner's office they searched the bayou banks in close proximity for any possible clues. They were awaiting the medical examiner because they could not legally move the body until that agency's representative was present. They were also waiting on the dive team because that unit has flat bottomed boats and metal and wire mesh litters to recover bodies with. The detectives hoped that the Homicide Gods would smile upon them with a gift as to who either the dead man or his killer was. Crooks have lost their wallets and left other damning evidence at scenes before. The investigators deputized all the officers at the scene as well as a wrecker driver and a deputy constable who just stopped by to gawk and scratch. Their searching, however, proved fruitless, except everyone involved in the search got numerous chigger bites.

While the detectives were waiting on the medical examiner and the body transport van to haul the remains to the morgue, a news reporter approached them. He advised them that one of the local news helicopters was reporting that there was a second possible body in the bayou one hundred yards or so further upstream.

The two investigators hiked the distance and confirmed the discovery. Now they had a double homicide investigation dropped upon them on an otherwise quiet Saturday afternoon. The two investigators had completed several hundred murder investigations between the two of them, but what they saw at the second scene that day caused them to stare in disbelief. There were no fewer than four junior-high-aged kids standing on the bayou bank near the second body. Each of the kids had crab lines in the water and dip nets at the ready as they caught crabs attracted to the rotting human carcass. The kids were regularly pulling in blue crabs and throwing them into a waiting ice chest.

The detective known as Lumpy had been raised in the Cloverleaf/Channelview area. Upon reviewing the crime scene he made the rather profound statement, "Only in Cloverleaf, Texas would people chum for crabs with a dead body. There ain't no other place else quite like it on earth—and we should thank God for that fact."

FIVE

··

DEMONICA THE HE/SHE

Demonica Dearly began life as Darren Dowling. At the age of twenty-six he was a card-carrying tried-and-true transvestite that just knew he had to be a woman trapped in a man's body. Cross dressing and doing his level best to look the part of a woman was just not enough. His ultimate goal was to be totally transformed. He longed in his sick little fruitcake mind to become a beautiful woman. He'd been on hormone treatments for a good while and had breast implants. Before he had the chopping and rechanneling of a sex change operation he decided that he really needed to sire a child. That way his father could become a grandparent. Demonica found a woman (of sorts) that agreed she would bear his offspring for two thousand dollars. Their agreement was half up front and the remainder to be due after the child was three to four months of age.

The brood sow was pollinated according to the plan. The illegitimate get of a prostitute/transvestite cross was whelped at a county hospital (naturally) at the taxpayer's expense. By this time Darren Dowling had legally changed his name to Demonica Dearly. His offspring's birth certificate showed Demonica Dearly as the named father and Sophia Smithers as the birth mother. Demonica visited the child once or twice weekly and brought money, a few little gifts, and diapers on each visitation. When it came time to pay the final installment and to claim ownership of the bastard child—the brood sow balked. She refused to turn her baby over to the he/she's daddy for raising. The drag-queen-turned-baby-daddy went "ape-shit" crazy and grabbed up a butcher knife.

The baby's mother lived in spite of her multiple wounds. The baby's maternal grandmother, however, did not survive her injuries. Darren/Demonica was identified by Sophia Smithers and he was readily identified and arrested. He claimed no knowledge as to how either of the ladies had been injured.

The investigators that were assigned to the double stabbing/DOA case were named Lewis and Andrews. The pair of detectives made the scene and went to the hospital before searching for the suspect and missing baby. They found Demonica and the child at the child's paternal grandfather's home. The transvestite could not explain the three minor cuts on his left hand. Blood tests with DNA would later prove positive for his blood on the baby's grandmother's clothes. The investigators got a *consent to search* from the suspect and went through the house he lived in with his father. They found no bloody clothes therein, but he/she/it apparently could not bear to part with a $250 pair of size 14E British Knight tennis shoes. Both the blood of the baby's mother and grandmother was found upon them.

The suspect's bedroom walls were covered with glamour shots and some nude photos of itself. He apparently would tuck his genitalia up under himself when he posed for the wannabe pin-up girl photos. When Lewis got home from work on the night of the killing he was trying to explain all that went on that day to his wife.

His spouse listened open-mouthed to all this and asked if the defendant's boobs looked real in the photos and how big they were.

Lewis got slapped on the top of his bald head after he said, "Hell Honey, if they hadn't been black I wouldn't have been able to tell them from yours."

She would have slapped him twice as hard if she knew that he related their conversation to anyone who would listen around the coffee pot the next morning at work. The suspect in this case would ultimately plead guilty to murder charges and received a thirty five year sentence. He died in prison from AIDS, a disease that many in the criminal justice system sometimes called death by lethal injection.

SIX

....

DISCRETION IN ACTION

"The difference between a police officer and a cop is that a police officer knows how to use discretion when dealing with people. A cop is just an idiot that uses the law to lord over people by just going by the book. You can make friends out there for the department, even on traffic stops. Telling someone they need to slow down or get their inspection sticker renewed—and then cutting them loose—wins friends in the community. There has always been plenty of trash on the streets to hammer. Take care of the decent people—they are the people you are supposed to protect. If they act stupid when you stop them, then write them up. Use your traffic stops for probable cause. Do you smell alcohol or marijuana? Now, you can search or do a sobriety test. Discretion is the mark of a professional. Anybody can be a cop."

Sgt. Charlie Boone, 1974
Houston Police Academy

With the trial lawyers wanting to sue everyone possible, police agencies attempt to codify their rules and regulations as much as possible. That way they can attempt to claim your actions were outside of the scope of your employment and sever themselves from any lawsuit if possible. Police work is really nothing but a people business. As such, rules that are hard and fast and inflexible don't always make much sense. A policeman's job requires him to be able to adapt to situations as they arise. The unwritten policy of Houston's Homicide Division has always been to help out the good citizens whenever possible and piss on the crooks in society every time you can. This policy is the same in many jurisdictions, but nobody will ever admit to it existing. There are a few weak sisters that have (and still do) work in the Homicide Division but they are not the norm, thankfully.

There is a departmental manual that dictates the procedures to be followed while working Homicide. For the most part the investigators working there have never bothered to open the books that were issued them. There are, thankfully, many detectives that claim the Standard Operating Procedural Manual should be relegated to bathroom reading.

Sometimes a little coaching is in order to ensure that all needed elements regarding the legality in a shooting are there when dealing with good citizens or homeowners. It is unfortunate but from time to time someone will talk themselves into a felony charge when it is not really necessary. This is another reason that typewritten statements are best. If you do an audio recording, the rattled shooter may blurt out something that will get him indicted. All he or she needs to say is, "I didn't have a choice. I was afraid he was going to kill me." If they say, "We fought and I took his gun away from him. I just lost it and I guess I really didn't have had to shoot him," then criminal and civil liability problems rear their ugly head.

When a business owner responds to a burglar alarm at night and shoots someone inside his fenced-in yard he is not automatically justified in doing so. Trespassing is not grounds for using deadly force. He can get charged if he says the wrong thing. If, however, the business or home owner puts in his statement that he saw the suspect exit his home or the front door of his business, his actions have now been justified under the law. Should the party in question be able to say that he saw some shiny object in the suspect's hand that he thought was a weapon his position is further strengthened. It may have only been a screwdriver—but as long as the shooter thought it was a weapon at the time it will float on through the system. In Texas, the shooting of burglars at night is completely legal. The shooting of trespassers, however, will get your hide nailed to the barn door.

The following is the statement of a homeowner who shot a neighborhood crack head who chose the wrong location to play peeping tom. The weapon of choice was a 20-gauge pump shotgun loaded with #8 birdshot. At close range it vaporized the crack monster's lower jaw and most of his tongue. The neighborhood where the shooting transpired was named Scenic Woods. The population therein was lower socio-economic and almost all black. Nothing scenic, however, has ever been found to exist in that neighborhood.

The investigators at the scene decided they did not want to charge the homeowner. They called it as a justifiable shooting, and besides, the injured party was a lower form of life on his best day. They called the intake section of the District Attorney's Office and spoke to the chief prosecutor on duty. They reviewed the facts with him or her and were advised that they did not want to accept charges on the shooter. The next call was to the homicide duty lieutenant and advised him what they had. Then if the investigator on the phone has any grey matter going for him or her they ask who is available for statements. He will pick out someone who will do the job right and speak to them. He will request that specific detective take the shooter's statement and tell him how he wants it constructed.

That way it's put together in such a way that it will go through the system without problems. You don't build a house without a good foundation, and you construct a case so it will hold up under scrutiny. You never know who the shot-up suspect will be found to be related to down the line.

See the following statement for an example of how such a statement is constructed properly to cover all the bases.

```
State of Texas        Date: 01-15-20XX
County of Harris      Time:  1930 Hrs
```

My name is Richard K. Simpson. I live at XXXX Artimus in Houston, Texas. I am a black male 58 years old, having been born 5-12-50. My Texas driver's license number is 1567XXXXX, and my social security number is 437-XX-XXXX. I am employed by Yellow Cab of Houston at XXXX Hayes Street. My home phone number is 713-552-XXXX and my work phone number is 713-XXX-XXXX.

This evening after work I had been sitting in my easy chair for about five minutes when my 13-year-old daughter screamed from her back bedroom. I ran to her room and she said there was a man outside trying to get in through her bedroom window. I grabbed up my pump shotgun from the hall closet and ran

out into the backyard. Outside of her bedroom window and inside my four-foot high
chain link fenced yard I confronted a black
man I have seen around the neighborhood for
about the last year. I do not know his name
but I've heard he is a crack head and is
dangerous. I have only spoken to him once
and that was when he was trying to camp on
the bayou bank right behind my house. I told
him that my property line went all the way
to the middle of the drainage bayou behind
my house and that I was not leasing it to
him to live on. He finally moved after he
just stood there for a good while just glar-
ing at me. I don't think he ever said a word
to me on that occasion.

Today when I confronted the man in my
backyard he had a backpack slung over his
left shoulder. When I confronted him he
reached into that backpack. I thought he was
reaching for a gun and I shot him one time.
He pulled his hand out of the bag so I did
not shoot him again, even though I pumped
another round into my shotgun. The man I had
just shot turned and walked across the yard
and down my drive. I followed after him until he left my property. I never shot him a
second time because he never again reached
into the bag he had slung over his shoulder.
If he had stuck his hand in there again I
would have shot him again. I have been told
by neighbors that the man is an ex-con and

is dangerous, and from what I have seen of him I believe it.

I am fifty-six years old and I have both high blood pressure and diabetes. Today when I confronted the man I thought was he was breaking into my home. He was inside my fenced in backyard. I shot him because I knew in my mind he was reaching for a weapon so that he could do me harm. Under the same set of circumstances I would be forced to do the very same thing again.

Richard K. Simpson

Sworn before me the undersigned authority this 15th day of January 20XX.

—

Notary Public in and for the State of Texas

The case was referred to the Harris County Grand Jury without charges. The investigators felt no crime had been committed and it was simply a shame that the suspect had not died at the scene. That way the county hospital district would not have to spend tons of money putting a worthless piece of street trash back together. Two days after the shooting incident the shooter/homeowner called the sergeant who had taken his statement. Sergeant Mike O'Brien crafted Simpson's statement so that it justified Richard Simpson's shooting of the peeping tom. Mike would later claim it was the same sort of statement he would have put together for his own dear father had himself been the one wielding the scattergun on the afternoon in question.

Mister Simpson, on the night of the shooting, requested and was given a photocopy of the statement he had just given. After mulling over the facts of the case in his head for a day or so Simpson took that copy of his statement to a criminal defense attorney that he knew. Simpson told the old detective-sergeant, "That lawyer sat down and read my statement and asked me: 'Is this Sergeant O'Brien a friend of yours?' I told him no, that I'd never met you before that night. Then that lawyer, he tol' me: 'This man (Sergeant O'Brien) most definitely is a friend of yours whether you know it or not.'"

Another example of discretion is the following. Harmon and Clanton made a shooting/DOA scene at Clayton Homes (a hell-hole government housing project) just east of downtown Houston. A well-known dirt bag passed on to that big dope house in the sky. The dead man was named Juanito Mata and he was both a junky and a thief. There was a single witness named Rosa

Hernandez that admitted to Clanton that she had seen the murder. She was ten years old and was being raised in the projects by a single mom. Rosa knew both the victim and suspect and saw the whole killing from beginning to end. The murderer was a street level drug dealer from a notorious and vicious family of heroine dealers.

If Clanton and Harmon filed murder charges on the suspect, then his ruthless family would, in turn, kill both the child witness and her mother. This would make an example of them in the community and bolster the reputation of the dope dealers. Rather than endanger the witness and her mother, the investigators chose to not list Rosa or her information in their report. The dead man was trash and no loss to society. The killer was trash, and he too was on a fast track to Hell. The case in question remained uncleared. The child and her mother lived. The detectives' actions did not follow the letter of the law. They did, however, protect the lives of two innocent people that night.

It only took Juanito's killer six months to get his own ticket to Hades punched in another drug deal. Deaths of persons such as Juanito Mata or the man that in fact killed him are often called OSHA Killings by Homicide investigators. If you are either a dope user or dealer, getting killed is nothing more than an occupational safety hazard. Sometimes little Johnny from middle America goes out to buy dope and gets himself killed by the street drug predators. It simply goes with the territory and may be the price of admission into the dope realm. The persons that reside therein are not the salt of the earth—they in reality are more like something that should be scraped from the bottom of your shoe.

Thus ends the lesson on a policy that no agency will ever admit exists. Discretion in the people business, however, needs to reside in the realm of professional law enforcement. Your position therein is to take care of the decent people. In today's world, chiefs of police are brought in from outside of an agency so they owe allegiance only to the man or woman who appointed them. Their orientation does not include discretion. In fact they generally attempt to limit its use through their love of rules and regulations. They lower the entry standards and limit the troops' ability to use discretion. Unfortunately this concept has found its way into the ideology of American policing. Ask any member of the International Association of Chiefs of Police.

....

SEVEN

DO-DO HAPPENS

Herbert Moore was an evening-shift big city homicide detective. One day he went out and bought himself one of those fancy new Glock 9mm high-capacity pistols.

The Glock company began the novel concept of making handguns with plastic composite frames. These guns are very light in weight and can carry and fire as many as nineteen rounds of ammunition at a time. Even more unusual was the fact that these pistols have a safety on the front of their triggers. Rumor had it that Herbie Baby would take a drink now and then, but it is unknown if he'd had a snort on the night in question.

Following dinner one night, and after returning to the Homicide office at 1200 Travis, he felt the call of nature. Upon entering the stall of his choice he drew his brand new pistol and hung it on the coat hook inside the stall door. Some minutes later when he chose to leave the stall he grabbed the pistol's grip and chose to unlatch the stall door at the same time. Unfortunately when he lifted up on the pistol in an attempt to take it off the coat hook, the door was already swinging open. He lifted the pistol and bumped the fancy safety and trigger system against the metal hook. This caused the handgun to discharge into the ceiling. The firing of the weapon caused it to recoil back into his hand. Herbie then hurriedly attempted to unhook the weapon's trigger guard from the coat hook on the still free-swinging stall door. He would then again attempt to unhook the trigger guard by lifting up on the weapon as the door swung back and forth. The gun's trigger would continue to make contact with the coat hook and the weapon would discharge and recoil back into his hand again and again. This procedure would repeat itself a total of four times as the man panicked and feverishly attempted to unhook his duty weapon from the wildly swinging bathroom stall door.

Four rounds in total were fired into the bathroom's plaster ceiling. Luckily there was nobody standing at the line of urinals directly across from the stalls in question. Everybody got a big laugh out of the situation (except Herbie who was always a bit full of himself anyway). The next morning all manner of signs began getting plastered all over the men's room entry door. Some read:

Warning—Free Fire Zone or **Unload All Weapons Before Entering.**

On the second day full-sized silhouettes from the pistol range began to appear taped up on the men's room walls. They all bore captions that were quotes from either John Wayne or Dirty Harry movies. They read, **Fill your hand Herbie, Well, Herbie are you feeling lucky today punk?** and **Bold talk for a four-eyed fat man, Herbie.** For several weeks there was any number of tourists (both men and women) that came from City Hall (and from all over the city as well) to see the bullet holes in the 6th floor Homicide Division men's room ceiling. The jokes finally culminated with the presentation of a t-shirt that was presented to Big Herbie at the annual Homicide Division's Christmas party. It bore the following legend.

Det. Herbie Moore
Famous Shithouse
Killer from Texas

....

EIGHT

DOCTORS OF DEATH

Glenda Faye Mitchell was a trashy barfly of a woman married to a man named Thomas Mitchell. Tom was a forty-two-year-old widower when he was injured on the job as a City of Chicago police office. Two years after he was medically retired he moved to Houston and took a job as a uniformed supervisor with a national security company. He met and married Glenda Faye and readily supported her and her three children. Glenda had been a barmaid at a place Tom frequented after work. Unfortunately for him he could not get the beer joint lifestyle out of her. It should have been a dead giveaway to him that she had three kids by three different men, and that Glenda hadn't bothered to marry the last two of her babies' daddies. All of the guys in question however had pretty good jobs and were on the hook for child support.

While Tom was off working, Glenda met up with a recently released ex-con loser named Johnny Ray Collard. Johnny Ray was a good dancer and a good times guy to party with. He also had good dope. Glenda wasted no time in packing up one day and moving both she and her kids in with Johnny Ray and his parents. Three weeks into her new relationship Collard became paranoid behind his increased dope use and started beating the hell out of Glenda. Tom had never changed the locks on his house, so one evening he walked back into his rent house after work and found his estranged wife and three step-kids waiting on him. She got down on her knees and begged for forgiveness. He stupidly took her back in but did not live long enough to regret it.

One week to the day after reuniting with Miss Glenda, Tom came home to find Johnny Ray in his living room, brandishing a pistol. Tom sent his step-kids to their rooms and then ordered the white trash doper out of his house. Collard shot Tom Mitchell three times in the chest with a .25-caliber Titan brand mouse gun. Tom died on the floor of the living room. Johnny Ray then proceeded to tear Glenda's clothes off her scrawny frame before he stuck the mini-gun against the side of her head. Then he sent her to the big honky-tonk in the sky. To round things out, in a blaze of glory our hero Johnny Ray shot himself in the side of the head. When the police and paramedics arrived the murder suspect was the only adult on the scene that was not dead. They packed his sorry carcass off to Ben Taub hospital where he was taken into surgery. His gunshot wound entry was at a shallow angle and the doctors said his recovery was certain and that he unfortunately would show little (if any) bad effects from the injury or surgery.

The Detectives that made the scene were named Harmon and Forrest. They interviewed the floor doctors in the Neurological Intensive Care Unit. One of the doctors interviewed had been present at the surgery and agreed it was a shame that the killer was going to be the only party to survive. The detectives went on to tell how the crook had been in prison most of his adult life and would continue to be a drain on the taxpayer until he turned up his toes. One of those doctors commented, "Yeah, it is a shame that a no-good drug-abusing bastard like that will go on and live. The world would be a better place if this piece of white trash would somehow die in his sleep tonight."

Somehow a miracle occurred that night inside the Harris County Hospital District. The suspect, Johnny Ray Collard, somehow died in Ben Taub Hospital from his non-fatal gunshot wound. The pathologist who posted Johnny Ray's sorry carcass the next morning was a friend of the detectives in question. He listed the cause of death as a suicide brought about by a self-inflicted gunshot wound to the head. The final ruling was suicide. Several years later while out on a deer hunt, the good Dr. Robert Jacobs (from the morgue) confided in Forrest that he really did not know how Johnny Ray died. It was, however, his professional opinion that justice somehow had been served and that the world was a far better place. He would not elaborate. Dr. Bob would only laugh and chew on his cigar.

NINE

....

DOG TO THE RESCUE

Within the Houston Police Department there used to be a division of officers that rode three-wheeled motorcycles and worked only traffic. They worked both day and evening shifts and really did no actual police work at all. The officers had a corner they had to direct traffic on for an hour or so a day and their ticket quotas were to write either ten parking tickets or two moving violations daily. Other than that they were basically left to their own devices. Many of these officers did not have a clue about how to do even the bare minimum amount of actual police work. These guys knew how to fill out an accident report, but some of them did not even know how to fill out an offense report recovering a stolen vehicle. The unit was called Point Control officially, but the officers throughout the department called it Three Wheelers.

There was an Arab-run convenience store called the Baby Giant that was located at the intersection of West

Dallas and Heiner streets just a couple of blocks west of downtown. It sat just behind or just south and east of a large and dilapidated government housing project called Allen Parkway Village. Closing time at that store was eight o'clock at night because the chances of an armed robbery occurring increased exponentially if the store stayed open any later. On one Thursday night, Abdul closed the door for the night as usual, but made a tragic mistake. When he left the business he locked the dead-bolt between the double glass doors, but he failed to engage the top and bottom pins in one of the doors. About eight fifty one that night some of the local street urchins pulled on the front doors and they parted like the Red Sea for Moses. Everything they found therein was then declared free for the taking. The word spread like a wind-whipped grass fire and the projects empties out. It must have looked like a flock of ducks descending on a June bug convention. The interior of the store was stripped of beer, wine and food. Whatever was not stolen was broken.

Two Point Control officers pulled into the parking lot of the Baby Giant store to finish their paperwork on a car wreck investigation they had just made. They onviewed the looting of the convenience/grocery store and had not a clue what to do. Instead of calling out on a *burglary in progress* they dropped an *assist the officer* call. An *assist the officer* call meant they are in trouble and need a cavalry charge to extract them from a bad situation. When the first of the patrol units arrived at the scene they found the two Point Control officers inside the building. The traffic cops had seven juvenile burglars hemmed up in one corner of the store at gunpoint. One of the Three Wheelers was holding a chrome plated sawed-off single-shot shotgun with a pistol grip on the thieves while the other would-be cop was reading them their rights. The patrol officers sacked up the prisoners and transported them to the Juvenile Division for the Point Control guys.

TEN

....

DON CARTER

I just knew that I was going to get indicted before I got off my first rotation as a probationary officer. I'd been paired with the meanest old man on the face of the earth. His name was Don Carter and I was sure that there was nothing that he would not do or say. He was any crook's worst nightmare, as well as a horror story waiting to happen as far as I could see it. Don was old as dirt and worked the 1500 to 2300 hour shift because he would shoe horses in his off time. I felt sure that he bent the iron horse shoes in his teeth and kicked horses' butts if they didn't act right. He set the ground rules with me real quick. It was his car, his radio and I was his rookie. He didn't make me call him Bwana White Bossm but that was most likely because he hadn't thought of it yet.

Don would tell somebody something once and then put hands upon them if they did not comply immediately or wanted to argue. If a prisoner got smart-mouthed he was lucky if he didn't just get the piss slapped out of him. When he open-handed someone it sounded like a .22-short going off. This training officer was only the second person I ever saw that could draw blood by slapping someone with an open hand. He actually split the skin by just slapping someone across the face.

I will never forget our first day on patrol together. We were riding out of the Central station. It was an early spring day and we had the windows rolled down. We had just signed on (gone on duty) and Don asked me what type of pistol I was carrying. I told him a blued steel Smith & Wesson model 19. He asked to see it, so I handed it to him. We were in front of the Rice Hotel in downtown Houston just after three in the afternoon. He looked at my shiny new revolver and he said, "Looks nice and clean." Then he stuck it out the window and pointed it straight up in the air. He proceeded to crank off three rounds of 125-grain hollow-points into the sky. Next, Carter threw my pistol back into my lap and told me, "Shoots good too. Never hand your pistol to anyone, kid."

A pair of sheep shears graced his briefcase as well as a pair of lineman's pliers. When a hippy-type was arrested for possession of any kind of dope, they forfeited their treasured hair piece. In the course of a street investigation and a prisoner needed questioning, the pliers were applied to the inside of their nose or to an ear lobe.

Carter claimed he'd never had a dirt bag lie successfully to him yet. You've got to keep in mind that Don Carter was an aggressive crime fighter type and he looked upon it as a bad week if he could not get into at least one good fist fight.

Somehow I made it through the first phase of my probationary period without getting dragged before either a state or federal grand jury. Needless to say I was much relieved. There was (surprisingly) only one Internal Affairs investigation complaint that I had to address while riding with him. Some pothead claimed my partner shoved him down in the back seat of our patrol car and cut off his pony tail. I'd been riding with Don on the day stupid got arrested. I did not recall ever seeing anything like the complainant described transpire during the period of time he was in our custody. How he got that bald spot on the back of his head is unknown to me still to this day.

It was not until several years had passed from my first days in Radio Patrol that I figured out how I and other rookie officers had been pigeon-dropped by our trainer Don Carter. I had about four or five years on the street when I happened to be in the company of some other officers talking shop. Carter had just retired from the department and had taken a job with the district attorney's office as an investigator. We were all discussing having ridden with the old fossil and were recanting

SGT. BRIAN FOSTER

horror stories from having to ride with the man under duress. One of the guys present made the comment, "You know, the whole time I rode with Don Carter I found more Reds (Seconol) on street turds than I'll likely find the whole rest of my career." Everyone present agreed that the same was true in their Carter training time also.

The realization struck me like a kick to the cods. The events when we made Seconol arrests were always the same. They came about during traffic stops. It did not matter if it was a car load of scummy folks or a lone bottom feeder. Don would have initiated the traffic stop and go up and obtain the traffic violator's driver's license. He would take the guy's driver's license and go back to the patrol car to check wants and warrants on the driver. He would tell me to keep an eye on the soon-to-be-drug defendant and to check the car out for further violations or contraband.

I would walk up to the car and shine my flashlight inside it. Therein I would spot a Red on the dashboard, transmission hump or floorboards. We then had probable cause to arrest everyone inside the car and to search it for any other possible contraband or stolen property. He would plant the drugs and whatever rookie he was riding with would be his unwitting accomplice. The drugs had always been in plain sight. What's more, it was always the junior officer that spotted the dope and initiated the arrest. The rookie could always pass a polygraph any day regarding what had occurred. The senior partner had been in the patrol car or just standing in close proximity at the time that the dope was discovered. He had been called back to the violator's car to assist in the felony arrest. Don was pure as the driven snow, and could not be accused of planting any dope. He'd simply backed up his rookie partner who spotted the drugs while they were making a routine traffic stop. The more I reflected upon it, I recalled that the only *attaboy's* I got from the man were on those occasions I found drugs that he had most likely planted. After comparing notes with all those other officers that day I began to wonder just where Carter got all those pills.

ELEVEN

....

DON'T CLOSE YOUR EYES

I rode with Jimmy Gray out of the Central Station. When we got into the patrol car that first day he asked me, "Okay White Boy, what you want me to teach you?" I told him I needed to learn how to be a cop and how to stay alive. He told me that wasn't a problem and that he might be able to give me some insight into life in The Ward. In Houston, low-income or blighted areas are called The Ward by cops. The term is a holdover from a hundred years ago when political districts were give numbers like the First Ward and such. Now they are called council districts. I asked him if I should call him Blood, Homey or Brother Man. He told me that I wasn't his "damned honky" brother, but rather his green-eyed cousin. I thereafter called him Uncle Jimmy (later short-ed to Unc) and he called me Cuz.

The last time I saw Unc alive it was in the springtime. We were sitting in the sun on his front porch drinking mint tea. His mother (who had to have been in her mid-to late 80s at the time) had told him that mint tea made from fresh picked mint would purify your blood. I gave him a copy of my first book and we visited. I asked him about his strangest experiences while on the police department and the following is what he related to me. He would not tell me who the players were or where it happened. In all honesty it worked out better that way. The names of all parties involved have now been sealed forever in a concrete coffin liner in a place called Barrett Station, located just outside of Crosby, Texas.

"Now listen up good Cuz 'cause you ain't gonna hear no shit like this many times in your life. What's more, there ain't nobody that can make stuff up like this. Now that you're a big time writer I want you to put this down. My first day on the street as a Houston police officer and the first call of my police career was a humdinger. I was riding night shift on the east end with an old-time shooter.

I will not mention the man's name 'cause you know him and he is still alive. I'd never met the man before that night, nor had I even heard his name before roll call that night. We S.O.'d (signed on the radio) and immediately were given a burglar alarm call. I was riding in the passenger seat and my trainer drove the last half block to the warehouse with the headlights off. We pulled up and were just exiting the car when an eighteen-year-old burglar came out the back door and fired a round at us. I heard the pop from the crook's .22 pistol and I ducked. I then heard the God-awful blast of my partner's .44-magnum pistol go off—Blam.

Homegrown the Burglar done slammed to the concrete floor inside the doorway of the building he'd just exited. I swear to God it looked just like he was on a string and got jerked off his feet. He was half in and half out of the building. We approached and my partner was a bit in front of me and to my left. The burglar was lying on the floor and his pistol was about two feet from his right hand. He looked up at us and my partner told him, 'Don't you close your eyes Nigga or you're gonna die in the dark.' Then he shot that piece of shit once more in the chest just for good measure.

My trainer still had his gun in his hand when he turned and looked me full in the face and asked, 'You gotta problem with that?' I just kinda shrugged my shoulders and said 'Not me.'

The case went to a grand jury and they had a bunch of questions about them concrete chips being in that dead man's back. The big .44 bullet went clean through the crook and splattered into the concrete underneath him. I told them I saw a gun in the burglar's hand as we approached and that my partner fired and protected both of our lives. I testified that I did not fire the first time because I was caught off guard and was scared. I went on to tell them that I was not in a position to take a shot when we approached the wounded man. In those days if or when you shot a burglar nobody really cared much anyhow.

Now put that story in your next book, White Boy. There ain't nobody gonna be able to verify my story either way. I've been diagnosed with cancer of the pancreas. Them damn fool doctors are trying to feed me a line about treatments and cures and some such bull corn. I know that ninety-five percent of the people diagnosed with pancreas cancer are dead within ninety days. Most everybody with pancreas cancer don't even make it that long. Them doctors, they just wants to make their Jaguar and BMW payments offa radiating me and pumping me full of them chemotherapy chemicals. Let somebody else pay for the boob jobs on all them doctor's wives and girlfriends. I know I got me maybe one or two good months ahead of me. There are a couple of things I want to do and a few people I want to see before I go. After that I just need for 'em to make me comfortable.

Cuz, now you got you one hell of a story to run with. I know you can do it justice and put it down like you're supposed to. That way you can shock the ever-lovin' hell outta all them liberal folks. Them Rednecks is gonna love you forever for this one too. Everybody that reads it will know its true, but caint (can't) nobody prove it is for sure one way or the other except me. Let 'em dig me up and put me in front of another grand jury. I'd tell *them the same thing again anyway if I could. They couldn't prove it happened no different way even if they wanted to."*

Jimmy laughed, telling me to be prepared because I might have to go before a grand jury after writing this story, and he was just sorry he wouldn't be around to see that happen. He said it was just too good a police story to get buried with an old man and he said he wanted me to record it.

"After all," the old man chuckled, "You're not a bad guy—for a white man." That was the only time since I'd met Jimmy that he'd referred to me as anything but a white boy.

TWELVE

....

ELECTRONIC SURVEILLANCE

It is now very common for undercover narcotics transactions to be either audio- or videotaped by the police.
That way, there is no room for questions when those
transactions are presented as evidence at a trial regarding what was said or done. What's more, if a suspect
admits guilt on camera it is always a slam-dunk case for
the prosecution. This same evidence is not always the
cop's best friend when things go south, and stuff hits the
fan. It can, though, at times be both highly embarrassing
and entertaining. You don't hear the word *police* yelled
too often, but mother***er gets called out a lot when
cops are running a warrant and under pressure. J.D. was
a cop with unreal street instincts. He was also a shooter.
He would (they say) walk into a lion's mouth just to get
the chance to shoot the big cat's tonsils off. There was
no grey as far as the man was concerned, just black and
white, like the silhouette targets at the police pistol
range.

His weapon of choice was a 12-gauge Remington 870 Wingmaster stoked with oo buckshot. He was, at one point in his life, a competitive skeet and trap shooter, but he sold his competition guns after his reputation as a man killer became noted by the media. In competition and on the street he carried the same type of weapon. His competition guns, however, had trigger jobs done on them. He was well educated and wrote his own statements following each of his shootings. He did not need the services of a police union lawyer. The shotguns he used while he was both in patrol and in the narcotics division were always unmodified riot guns. The shotguns he used in narcotics work were also issued weapons. The Houston Police Department does not think enough of their street officers to issue them long guns. All officers are also required to purchase their duty handguns and the ammunition they carry on duty.

Rodney Jefferson was a nickel and dime dope dealer. He got busted by a multi-jurisdictional task force on a small powdered cocaine sale. He was a second offender and wanted to play let's-make-a-deal really bad. He claimed he could turn some major league Jamaican dealers, and signed a court approved contract to do so. The details of that contract called for four purchases in excess of three ounces. Not a problem, said this pot-bellied street guy. There are two kinds of people in the dope trade: those that sell dope and those that claim they sell dope and rob people instead. The latter is what Rodney ran up on.

A six-ounce rock cocaine buy was set up off Interstate 10 in a downstairs motel room. The narcotics bust team was in the next room. A video camera and audio unit were inside a clock radio on the dresser of the room that Rodney was in. The bust team was next door inside another motel room watching the whole thing go down and recording it. Rodney was advised to stay in the area of the two double beds for safety's sake. That way they could watch him the whole time from the next room. The two Jamaicans walked into the room with a duffle bag. The first man through the door pulled out a handgun and pointed it at Rodney and the second gentleman pulled a short-barreled shotgun out of his bag and pumped a round into it. The man with the automatic pistol pointed it at Rodney and pulled the trigger a couple of times. It just snapped. The would-be killer stepped back and began racking the pistol's slide, attempting to get it to load a round into the chamber.

At that point in time, J.D. came through the motel room door but he was off-camera. He was heard to yell "*Police*". Rodney hit the floor. The pistol-wielding man hit the floor following the *whoomp* sound of J.D.'s issue shotgun. Then, the shotgun-wielding Jamaican appears in the left hand side of the screen. J.D. passed in front of the camera (shotgun in hand), followed by another *whoomp-whoomp* sound. J.D. walked back into the camera shot. Rodney was still lying on the floor between the two beds. J.D. asked Rodney, "Are there any other muthaf**kas in here?" Rodney answered back, "No you got'em all." J.D.'s supervisor then walked into the room and J.D. told him, "I had to take the shot." His supervisor answered in a tone that sounded none too believing, "Yeah, sure."

The video of the shooting made the rounds through the Homicide Division and the district attorney's office. It backed up that the suspects were armed and added some levity to the paper-pushing required in a police shooting. The official ruling by the Harris County Grand Jury was Justifiable Homicide. The final but unofficial ruling from the district attorney's office was a Justifiable Homicide—No Known Human Involvement.

THIRTEEN

....

FAST FOOD KILLS
OR
FRITO DE MUERTO

George Alred was Houston's first full-time police psychologist. His background and employment background was multi-faceted. While in college he worked the night shift in a hospital for the criminally insane. The federal prison system employed him for a few years as a consultant before he began teaching college in Texas. Somehow during this time period he was always able to maintain a successful family counseling practice on the side. The only exception to that was during the time he ran Houston's hostage negotiation team. Doctor George would admit that the most interesting personality types he ever ran across appeared during the twenty years he worked as HPD's staff psychologist.

His duties with HPD included the personality testing of police recruits, family and marriage counseling for departmental employees, and finally the formation and training of police officers into a hostage negotiation team. The team itself was composed of sworn police officers trained in the handling of hostile people and volatile situations. Their stated goals were to attempt to defuse dangerous situations and attempt to save lives in the process. Their areas of deployment might cover potential suicides to armed kidnappers and hostage takers. The unit by law is able to use wiretap equipment in order to open paths of communication with armed or dangerous subjects. Naturally they worked closely with SWAT teams, as many within their client base would often need the services of both units.

For the first couple of years that the hostage negotiation team existed George Alred helped train the negotiators and actually made hostage callout scenes along with the troops. His goal was to add his experience as a teaching tool regarding the dealing with certain personality types. His most startling scene had to do with an armed robbery suspect who sought to go out in a blaze of glory.

Rodney Allen Sonnier (pronounced sawn-yeah) was a thief. He was never known to have worked at any time in his pathetic life. Further, his life's goals as he stated them were, "gettin' by and gettin' high." He had been in and out of the criminal justice system all of his adult life. He was a two-bit crook and most all of his felonies were pled down to misdemeanor criminal convictions. As such, his only real permanent address could have been the Harris County Jail. He typified the police expression that "He was not worth the powder and shot it would take to blow him to Hell."

The name Rodney Sonnier was actually unknown on the streets of northeast Houston. That was because he was known to everyone thereabouts only as Dirty Red. Dirty Red was what is called a Redbone. He was a light-skinned black male of Louisiana heritage. He also has a red cast to his skin that looked like his bones glowed red, hence the term.

Rodney came to his end following a short police standoff and hostage-taking scenario. His passing was videotaped and is often used as part of training films for SWAT, military and law enforcement officers. The day before his death Dirty Red had been going about his daily foraging and stole a gallon of liquid methamphetamine from a neighborhood illegal drug manufacturing operation. With such a find our subject and his girlfriend simply sat around her kitchen table shooting speed, watching TV and playing cards. After a day or so of this he decided he needed a fried chicken fix.

The closest such dining establishment was located on Jensen Drive not far from Sweet Thang's apartment. He procured two orders of yard bird to go and when he arrived home he counted his change. His girlfriend said he began to rant and rave that he had been short-changed a total of one dollar and forty seven cents. Dirty Red dug out his stolen model 10 Smith & Wesson revolver and a pocket full of bullets. He stormed back to the chicken joint to set things straight. We are not talking about an orderly and rational minded individual here. Streetwise, yes indeed—but rational, no way in Hell.

The neighborhood in question was and still is extremely high crime in nature. As such, cash-only businesses in the area (such as the fried chicken establishment in question) are often forced to hire armed security guards to ward off armed robbers. Such was the case with Rodney's targeted site. Red marched into the eatery and immediately walked up to the Nigerian security guard. He put his gun to the guard's head and took his duty weapon. Still holding the guard at gunpoint he began to scream and yell at the counter help, demanding his money back that they allegedly had stolen from him. He next shot out a window to get everyone's undivided attention. A car sitting at the drive-in window had a full view of Rodney's antics and simply drove off. The driver went a block down the street and placed a 911 call about the robbery in progress.

The restaurant sat off by itself and patrol units quickly set up a perimeter. Rodney saw what was unfolding around him and his street animal brain quickly formulated a plan of his own. He was going to either get away completely or go out in a blaze of glory. SWAT was notified by the watch commander and the hostage negotiation team was similarly called out. The patrol officers at the scene tried to get Rodney's attention by calling out to him on their car's public address system. They advised him that they had the place surrounded and that he needed to give up. Rodney answered their demands by turning off the interior lights of the store and shooting at the police cars.

All his actions succeeded in doing nothing other than breaking a couple of store's plate glass windows and scaring the hell out of everybody inside the store. The hostage negotiation team showed up and tried to open telephone communication with the suspect. Red responded by tearing the business' phone out of the wall and throwing it outside of the building through a broken window. The outside parking lot lights came on at dusk and everybody in the store was well silhouetted.

Rodney was going for broke. He had the security guard remove his uniform shirt and he cut it into strips. With these strips he tied the guns to his hands. This way (in his street animal mind) he would not lose either gun if he was hit in an exchange of gunfire and he could take as many cops with him as possible. While he was binding the guns to his hands one of them discharged and the command post became concerned that one of the hostages had been wounded. The hostage negotiation team had one of the SWAT guys throw a phone on a cord through one of the broken windows and they called out on a bull horn for Dirty Red to pick up the phone. His response was pretty clear when the phone in question came flying back out of the broken window. A SWAT team sniper named Greg had just climbed up a pipe and had gotten onto a roof seventy-five yards north of the business when he was notified that it appeared the suspect was definitely up to something. They thought he might be getting ready to make a break from cover. The tactical boys could see the suspect had his hostages herded up into a corner and that he was doing something with one in particular.

Rodney came out of the building holding the security guard hostage directly in front of him. He had his model 10 Smith & Wesson cocked and up against the security guard's head. Red held the security guard's revolver up against the Nigerian's ribcage as he used the guard as a shield. His hope was to make it a block down the street and then he could turn and run up an alley. If he could make it that far he planned to ditch the hostage and cut over two blocks to his girlfriend's place. The sniper in the northern position (Greg) was asked if he had a clear shot.

Greg was going to have to make an off-hand shot just after climbing onto the roof, but he answered affirmatively. He had a clear head shot. He was told, "That's clear—You have the green light—let the man die." Greg answered, "The man is dead" as he pulled the two and a half pound trigger on his .308 caliber Remington model 700 rifle.

The only target Greg had was Rodney's head. He and his squad's team leader had just returned from an FBI SWAT training camp. There, they had been taught that a properly executed head shot could freeze all bodily motor functions. Their instruction was that all motor function in the body is controlled by the part of the brain directly in the back portion of the skull. If you have a shot from the front of your suspect, you want to shoot for the tip of his nose. The bone structure in that part of his face is lightest and will be less prone to deflect a bullet. Greg was holding on Red's nose when he pulled the trigger. Red, in his highly paranoid state, was snapping his head back and forth looking for the cops.

The 150-grain boat tail bullet hit him at the top and back portion of his ear and it was as if a light switch had been turned off. Dirty Red went rigid and locked up tight. He then fell like a telephone pole. When the rifle went off, three things happened. Rodney's head exploded, he dropped like a rock, and the Nigerian security guard hostage hit passing gear.

The hostage was still gaining speed two blocks from the scene when he was tackled by uniformed officers. The guns had to be cut from the cloth strips binding

Dirty Red's hands and it was noted that his trigger fingers were frozen in curved positions as if they were still resting upon the triggers. Both guns were double-action revolvers and the one to the hostage's head had been cocked. Neither one of the guns had discharged.

Dr. George Alred was present at this scene. He had been involved in directing the attempt to make contact with the suspect and resolve the situation. George decided that since the suspect was now beyond help, he should go up on the roof and attempt to comfort the sniper who had just had to take a human life. George was only on the roof for a total of sixty seconds when he came back down the ladder. A SWAT Team sergeant named Elton who was on-scene inquired "George is something wrong?"

Shaking his head and pointing toward the roof (while referring to the sniper) Alred answered, "He's laughing his fool head off and doing everything but jacking off!" Elton responded, "Yeah that may be true, but just who you want on the roof if you've been taken hostage?" George again pointed at the roof again and without hesitation replied, "That crazy son-of-a-bitch up there, that's who."

The end result of this fun-filled night in Houston's Fifth Ward was threefold. A canker sore in the form of Rodney Allen Sonier had been removed from the butt of humanity. The FBI's theory of freezing motor function with back of the head brain shots was proven up for the first time. Lastly the FBI was proven to be wrong when they said that a cocked Smith & Wesson revolver would always discharge when dropped on a hard surface.

The moral to this story is as follows. You can't believe everything your mother or your government tells you. Your mom lied to you, Sonny. You will not go blind if you keep doing that. You may need glasses later in life, but you *will not* go blind. The Feds either don't know everything or they will sometimes lie to you too.

FOURTEEN

....

FAUX PAS OF THE YEAR

Faux Pas (foe-paw) *noun. A word of French origin denoting a social blunder.*

The news media is always in a hurry. They need to get their story in before a deadline—following that, they move on to their next assignment or story. Investigative cops come to know that the media types will use you both *for* a story and *as* a story if they get a chance. Homicide investigators in particular deal with newspaper, radio and television reporters regularly. They also come to find out that those folks will pigeon drop and quote you even when you are talking "off the record." The Homicide Division for a while gave a plaque at their yearly Christmas party for that year's worst quote given to and reported by the press during that specific calendar year. Here are two award-winning stories.

Sergeant David Peak was sent out as a one-man unit to make a jumper scene in front of a posh Galleria area hotel. Had it been a low-rent district the Homicide Division would not have sent an investigator at all. All that would have been required would be just a crime scene unit and a patrol unit to make the offense report. The dearly departed, however, was an heir to a Colorado- and Kansas-based adult beverage fortune. The suicide itself was really somewhat less than remarkable. The lady left a rambling note before climbing over the rail of the 20th floor balcony. It was 7:30 a.m. when the aging debutante fell to the pavement in the outside lane of traffic on Westheimer Street. She was more than just a little worse for the wear. An urban cowboy in his jacked-up 4x4 pickup truck had to slam on his brakes to avoid running over the cadaver. The well-dressed goat roper was observed to pile out of his truck and stand there for a minute or so just looking at the battered human remains. He then grabbed both of the dead woman's ankles and matter-of-factly dragged her carcass over the curb and onto the sidewalk. Tex then got back into his trusty pickup and drove off into the sunrise. Everyone present was rather shocked by his actions but nobody had the presence of mind to get his license plate number.

David did his scene overview and found the suicide note inside the hotel room. The room itself had been locked from within by means of a safety chain. The patio door was still standing open. It was a straightforward high roller's suicide, a so-what-who-cares kind of case.

Sergeant Peak then gave his thirty- to sixty-second sound bites for the TV and radio reporters that were standing around. Then Dave went back to tying up his investigative loose ends before he could leave the scene and head to the morgue. Autopsy requests are filed with the medical examiner's office for specific tests of samples. If you are friendly with the M.E. investigators they will fill them out for you with a telephone request oftentimes (although you don't mention that part in your offense report).

A newspaper reporter came up and wanted some particulars in the way of information regarding the pickup driver, and what if anything was known about him. Dave knew the reporter and gave him the Reader's Digest condensed basic version. White male driver, brown hair and mustache, green Chevy 4x4 pickup truck. Drivers name and identity are both unknown at this time.

To his downfall, David also thought himself to be quite witty at times. He asked said reporter (who also drank at the same police bar as Sgt. Peak) if he now wanted the off the record story. Of course he did. Witty Dave went on to relate that the Rexall Ranger in question (drugstore cowboy) was either one of the most compassionate folks in town or he had to be the most cold-blooded S.O.B. in the county. He dragged Miss High Society out of the street for one of two reasons as far as the cops could figure. Either he did not want to be late for work, or he pulled her out of the street so that somebody else didn't come along and smash her flatter than a roadside beer can. Of course the off-the-record status of Dave's words was quickly forgotten.

Brother Dave's award was well earned and the selection committee's vote to make him the honoree was unanimous. His plaque was navy blue with large gold letters spelling out 19xx Faux Pas of the Year. Below this came his rank and name. Then the words **Smashed flatter than a beer can** appeared followed by a photo of the dearly departed covered by a sheet and a beer can that had obviously been run over.

Brooks Roberts was the next year's award recipient. He too had been called out to work a prominent person's death. This time however the investigation involved a delayed death. Homicide investigative types dislike delayed death situations because witnesses and evidence often no longer exist. In the case in point a female socialite was found dead in bed beside her high-roller husband. The fifty-year-old husband and his trophy wife had been out the night before dancing and drinking. They came home and hubby takes his Viagra and they make whoopee. Hubby said he awakened the next morning with an erection only to find Sweetie dead as a hammer and stiff as a carp. That was definitely tough luck in anyone's book. It gets worse when the high-powered attorneys show up just to protect everybody's rights and make themselves several grand before lunch. Then the mayor called the chief of police who in turn called the duty lieutenant for an update. Everybody knows a cop and everybody involved this goat f**k thought they were somebody special or wanted very badly to be one.

The only medical problem the slightly hung over husband could tell Brooks about was that Sweet Thing supposedly fell three days earlier and bumped her head on a curb. She went to their family doctor and was told to take Tylenol for the headache. Wifey was found to be clad only in a t-shirt. The couple's fancy clothes were found draped over a couple of chairs in the bedroom. There was no sign of a struggle or fight and no obvious injuries on the person of the dead woman. The physical part of the scene fit with what the grieving husband had to allow. The fact that there had been no less than three family disturbance calls at the house in the past eighteen months did not help anything, though. What is more, twenty-eight-year-old trophy wives with boob jobs, nose jobs and tummy tucks normally don't just up and die of natural causes too darned often.

The cadaver was shipped off to the county morgue for an autopsy and hubby and mega-bucks lawyers left the Homicide Division after hubby gave his statement. One of the high-powered lawyer types wanted to send the dead woman's remains to a private hospital and have the autopsy performed by a doctor of their choosing. The high rollers were really put out when their request was denied. Things got more interesting because it was a slow news day. The local media outlets set up such a clamor that it only lacked circus tents and fireworks displays. All that day the fifth estate was pounding on the dead woman's neighbors doors demanding interviews. *The public has the right to know* has always been their chant.

The next morning, before daylight, Brooks was on deck at the county morgue for the slicing and dicing ceremony. Autopsies are best conducted where natural light conditions exist. That is the reason that the better medical examiners offices have sky lights in their autopsy rooms. Certain poisons cause color charges upon some internal organs, and those colors are not visible under artificial lights.

The routine toxicology screens done upon the blood and tissue samples are for specific substances and the ability to do a visual screening culls several less common drug and poisons from the mix. When the dead woman's skull cap was removed (by a gnome-like morgue attendant) the cause of death became very evident. There had been an obvious injury to the back of the head and there was notable old bleeding in the area between the skull and the brain. The blood-to-alcohol level in the injury-produced blood was zero, while the dead woman's blood sample indicated .075. This even further bolstered the earlier injury story related by the husband and helped to clear him. The medical term for the woman's cause of death was a *subdural hematoma*.

The medical examiner's staff was impressed. They had never before had a cadaver with a nose job, a boob job, a tummy tuck and a butt tuck. The doctor "posting" the body proclaimed that the deceased was a trophy that you couldn't hang over the fireplace. The cause of death was ruled to be one of accidental injury.

Brooks Roberts was a West Texan from Coleman County. He had grown up in farming and ranching country and was straightforward and plain spoken. When he was later interviewed by a female newspaper reporter he was asked just how the complainant had slipped on a concrete drive. Roberts answered, "Woman, it had just come a sprinklin' rain after a good dry spell. When that happens, all the oil in the concrete floats up to the surface. Mate that light rain up with a pair of smooth leather-soled shoes and things get slicker'n snot on a glass door knob right quick."

He became immortalized behind his "slicker than snot on a glass door knob" statement in the next day's paper. His plaque had the standard Faux Pas of the Year Award legend across its top with the year it was earned. Brooks' name was on the next line and then came his quote, "Slicker than snot on a glass door knob," boldly displayed. At the bottom of the plaque was mounted a beveled glass door knob. Brooks' wife loved the award. He was not quite as impressed, but he bore up well under the ribbing.

....

FIFTEEN

THE FRIDGE FAMILY

The Fridge sisters came into the Southeast Station Family Violence Unit one July afternoon. They said they needed to make a report and claimed they wished to file charges. The two adults that entered the offices there at XXoo Mykawa Road were named Evonka and Uvonka Fridge. They brought with them Evonka's two-year-old child named Nakki Boo Fridge. They came directly from a shooting scene and never stopped to call the police. The only casualty in the incident was a five-year-old Chevrolet. The trio in question had been visiting a cousin at the Chez Orleans Apartments located at XXXX Sunflower Street. The Chez Orleans is such a hellhole that the locals call it the Jail House Apartments. This is because every window and door there has burglar bars covering them to keep the street animals from carrying the residents' belongings off. As the three Fridges were leaving the complex with Evonka's baby strapped into a car seat, Evonka's baby's daddy showed up in the parking lot, "Callin' me all kinda bitches and ho's." Ms. Evonka allowed that, "He ain't nuttin' but an ignorant ass dope fiend." When asked how long she had dated him she answered, "Four years and he's been steadily using crack the whole time." After she was counseled by the division's ultra liberal counselors she claimed she now feared for her safety as well as that of her child Nakki Boo and her sister Uvonka.

Evonka had been driving her Chevy Impala when her baby's sperm donor, Jovon Demonte, showed up outside her driver's window. The car was still in reverse when he appeared cursing and screaming. She stopped, and not to be outdone, began exchanging rude expletives with the man. When he pulled a gun out from under his shirt, she punched the gas pedal to speed away. Unfortunately in her haste to say rude things about Jovon's mother, Evonka left the car in reverse. When she slammed the accelerator to the floor she continued south and backed into the northwest corner of the 500 building of the rat-hole apartment complex.

When she and the other two Fridges drove off, Nakki Boo's daddy put a couple of 9mm bullets into the back of the car to get her attention. The projectiles were stopped by the four spare tires she had stored in the trunk of her car. The tires came to her by way of her new boyfriend Elvis who operated a car crusher for an automobile wrecking yard on Cullen Boulevard.

Evonka and Uvonka were both adamant about wanting to file charges when they came into the Family Violence Unit. Evonka advised that there had been prior problems with her former Stud Duck. She said he had been particularly irritating since they broke up a year earlier. "He put all my tires on flat, and calls me leaving all kinda nasty messages whenever he gets high, which is every day." Both of the Fridge sisters gave sworn affidavits and photos were taken of the bullet holes in the car's trunk. The fired bullets were recovered from the trunk, one of the trunk's floorboards and the other one from inside one of the spare tires. Charges were filed on the ex-con former boyfriend, who was ordered held without bond because he was on parole for possession of narcotics.

Jovon had to have a full-blown trial that ended with a twenty-five-year sentence being handed to him by the jury. Almost one year to the day following the shooting incident Uvonka came to her final end. The police were called to the government-assisted housing apartment complex where Uvonka and Evonka both lived under the HUD Section 8 mandate. Therein unmarried women with children and no husband or boyfriend living on site could get both an apartment and their utilities for $35 a month. It is a welfare brood sow's dream to live there and continue to procreate. Some of the residents there, when asked if they were employed, would tell you that they were on Child Support.

Anyway, one summer evening the police were called out to the apartment complex at XXXX Telephone Road regarding a mental case in the southeast parking lot near the manager's office. The exact words of the office manager when asked to describe the mental case's actions were "She be actin' a fool and shit!"

Uvonka was still outside and acting deranged when the blue suits arrived. She was walking around the apartment complex courtyard screaming a mixture of profanities and Bible quotes. It took several officers to wrestle her to the ground and handcuff her. About thirty seconds after she was pinned to the ground and handcuffed she calmed down and relaxed—and promptly stopped breathing. A full-blown investigation begins on any death in police custody situation. Those cases are reviewed by the Internal Affairs Division, the county's district attorney's office, as well as the Texas Attorney General's office. The Harris County Medical Examiner's Office ruled Uvonka's death was the result of a cardiac arrest related to cocaine toxicity.

After she was notified by the medical examiner about the cause of her sister's death, Evonka Fridge called the lead homicide investigator. She asked him what happened because she didn't understand what the M.E. investigator was trying to tell her about how "Sissy" died.

Albert Harmon tried his level best to explain the toxicology lab's findings to the woman, but to no avail.

The woman was later described by the crusty old cop as being as dumb as a whole box full of rocks and as ugly as a sack full of assholes. He finally shifted into low gear in an attempt to reach the lowest possible common denominator. She finally came to understand what happened when he told her, "It was one of two things. She either took too much dope, or got holda some bad dope and her heart done blowed up." Evonka now understood the situation and she thanked him profusely for his explanation. After the end of his conversation with Evonka the elderly Sergeant Harmon sat at his desk just shaking his head. He then turned to his partner and exclaimed, "You know the saddest thing about this whole situation is that these folks are able to procreate and vote."

SIXTEEN

....

FUNERAL HOME MISHAPS

The bulk of the funeral homes in Harris County, Texas are owned by one of two huge business conglomerates. They own the funeral homes, the flower shops and even the casket companies. Though they (the corporations) are, in my opinion, blood-sucking no goods that take advantage of people when they are their most vulnerable, their businesses are not mentioned in these pages. The big funeral conglomerates buy up old established funeral homes and the good citizens think the family that buried granny and granddad is still run by the Jones or Smith family instead of some national corporation. People are creatures of habit and the hardest traditions for us to break away from are education, wedding and funeral practices. The desks in our schools are lined up in rows running from the front of the room to the back of the room. This practice predated electric lights and the desks were originally lined up along the windows so that the kids could see what was on their desks. Electric lights however have been around for how many generations now?

The stories in this chapter are about just a couple of the mom-and-pop funeral homes that used to haul bodies to the Harris County Morgue. What's more they did it for free. The big corporations couldn't have been bothered with something they couldn't scam some widow out of a five hundred to eight hundred percent profit margin within a two to three day time period. The smaller funeral homes have always tended to be very above board and cheaper than the big outfits, and more service oriented. Their staff at most all levels in the businesses generally consists of family members rather than high turnover and under-paid hourly employees.

Until recently (the last eight to ten years) the Harris County Medical Examiner did not transport bodies. The cadavers that were to be autopsied somehow had to move from the place of death to the medical examiner's office. Instead the medical examiner's office had a deal worked out with the private funeral homes to haul the bodies for free. The funeral homes would also get the chance to contact the family as they did the notification of death for the medical examiner's office. That way the funeral homes got the first crack at hustling the funeral business as a payback for hauling the body for the county.

The program worked that way for more decades than anyone on the police department can remember. The medical examiner kept costs down because they did not have to staff a van to pick up stiffs. The funeral homes liked the program because they got to hustle additional business. Everyone won that way. Black funeral homes got to haul the black folks and white funeral homes got to haul the white folks. The couple of Hispanic funeral homes in town mopped up too. Black-owned funeral homes had a better chance of hustling a black person's family business than a white funeral home and vice-versa. Life was good. If you were the investigator at the medical examiner's office calling the funeral homes for body pick-ups you might get a couple of bottles of good whiskey at Christmas time if you put a certain funeral home at the front of the rotation more often than some others. Everybody benefited.

The following stories come from over a long period of time working in Houston's Homicide Division. There were a few funeral homes in that twenty plus year period that were operated by some rather unusual characters. They were not the norm at all, but for me not to pass along these wonderful stories would be unconscionable.

The Infernal Rest Funeral Home

When the Infernal Rest body car made your scene for a pick-up there was always a sideshow in the making. Their transport vehicle was a raggedy old custom van with the back seats removed and only the shag carpet left behind. The van came equipped with peeling paint, mag wheels and a spoiler on the back part of the roof like a Grand Prix style race car. Their choice in vehicles aside, the personnel that arrived on the scene in this contraption were known by the Homicide investigators and crime scene units as The Idiot and The Cripple.

The crime scene units got to see The Idiot and the Cripple most often. This is because homicide investigators are not sent out on all suicide and accidental death scenes. Crime scene officers, however, went out on all death scenes other than traffic accidents fatalities. The brains of this funeral home outfit was a short and scrawny dark-complexioned black male with a withered right arm. He was always under the influence of alcohol and wearing a white lab technicians coat with the left breast pocket full of tongue depressors. His sidekick was a huge hulking brute that stood about six and a half feet tall. That gentleman had a forehead that ballooned out and he never said much. The Cripple cursed and shrieked at this mammoth subhuman looking fellow non-stop. Everybody in the unit hated to see those two gentlemen pull up on the scene of their murders. The

Cripple was always polite enough to the cops, but they soon tired of the almost non-stop yelling at his assistant. Somehow the funeral home flunkies were always able to load the cadaver onto their gurney and haul it away (unsecured) into the back of the old custom van. They would then drive off to the morgue. You could hear The Cripple's squeaky voice yelling at The Idiot (above their loud exhaust) as they drove away from your scene.

Cloverleaf Funeral Directors

Lamar Random owned the company named Cloverleaf Funeral Directors that was located in northeast Harris County off of Interstate 10. That business adjoined his bar/pool hall. When you called the phone number listed in the phone book for the funeral home it rang inside both businesses. If Lamar was in the bar (as he usually was) he answered it there. There were two mute switches beside the phone so he could cut the volume off on either the TV or the juke box and conduct business from the end of the bar where he sat. Fancy the place wasn't, but if you wanted a no-frills or low bid funeral—then Big Lamar was your man.

Charles Ezzell Wicky died in Houston's VA Hospital following a lengthy illness (treated at taxpayers' expense). Though Charlie did not have the most sterling of reputations, his son and namesake Charles Junior was an even sorrier excuse for a human being. Bohemians tend to be hard workers, but many of them live strictly for a life of partying. Lying and cheating somebody out of either money or booze runs partying a close second as far as many are concerned. When Daddy Wicky passed on to the big beer joint in the sky, Junior got on the phone to see where he could dispose of his father's remains in the cheapest manner.

Lamar Random gave Charlie Jr. the lowest drive-out price of $585 for what was called a straight cremation. This consisted of simply picking up the body and the cremation process. He met the grieving son at the Veteran's Administration Hospital where all the necessary forms were signed. Charlie claimed to be so upset that he had forgotten his checkbook at home, but he promised to come by the funeral home the following morning at nine o'clock. By noon the next day when Junior hadn't so much as called, Lamar began hunting around for a certain grieving Bohemian.

When Lamar finally caught up with Charlie, the scum bag immediately began trying to weasel out of paying the whole bill. Random was told that Charlie simply didn't have enough money to pay the whole bill and the best he could do was to pay Lamar $385. Random told the scholar in question that he just needed to go around to other family members and take up a collection— because the money Charlie was offering would not even cover his (Lamar's) expenses. The younger Wicky balked at that and told Lamar, "That is as good as it is gonna get, and you need to get used to the idea because you (Lamar) are gonna do the job for $385!" Random was a straightforward kind of man. He told the dirt bag son that if he did not have the agreed upon $585 by noon the next day that he (Random) was going to transfer the moldering body of the late Charlie Wicky from the re-frigerated storage unit he now laid in to Charlie Junior's front porch. Charlie laughed and told Lamar, "You ain't got balls enough to do something like that, Nigger!"

Charlie Wicky (the younger) had not come by the fu-neral home, nor had he even bothered to even call by noon the next day. Lamar Random was a man of his word. At two that afternoon he put the remains of Charles Ezell Wicky on the doormat in front of his lov-ing Bohemian son's front door in Baytown, Texas. Now Lamar did have the decency to cover the body with a sheet and he left the cadaver on a backboard so that it would be easier to move the stiff if the low-life son wanted to move him inside and out of the weather. The Baytown detective that investigated that case was named Leonard Dill. He knew both the low-rent son as well as his alcoholic and now deceased father. Leonard told the district attorney that reviewed the case with him that he did not want to charge the undertaker. He knew that Wicky was trying to cheat the funeral home because he had a history of that sort of thing and had both a ton of criminal convictions and civil judgments against him. Besides, the undertaker had done only what he advised Charles Wicky Jr. he was going to do.

The case was referred to a grand jury without charges. Another funeral home unfortunately stepped forward and did the cremation for free. Lamar Random was ultimately charged with the misdemeanor offense of abuse of a corpse. He stepped up to the plate and paid his fine like a man. The judge asked him, after pronouncing sentence, if Lamar was sorry for what he had done. Lamar answered, "No Sir, and if I were put in the same set of circumstances again tomorrow I would probably do the same thing. That man was out to cheat me and I refused to let him. It is a matter of principal, Your Honor."

Charlie Wicky Jr. got his fifteen seconds of fame on television and he got exactly what he wanted—to beat somebody out of a free funeral. The lowest life son-of-a-bitch in the county won out. Then he went out and found an ambulance chasing attorney to file a civil suit against Lamar Ransom.

Grissom's Funeral Home

Steven Grissom was a cigar chomping fat man with greasy slicked back hair. He wheezed when he talked and always looked clammy and sweaty. The man looked the part of a pervert and in fact regularly was a patron of the street whores on Jensen Drive. He owned a funeral home on Houston's northeast side and he could be best described as being a slug of a man. To the amazement of the homicide investigators Steve never wore gloves when picking up the bodies at their murder scenes. Grissom's business sat on a piece of property that was worth millions of dollars. He inherited both the land and the business from his father. Steve, however, could never sell the business because he had so many civil judgments that had been levied against him. The judgments were the direct result of a lifetime of being a screw up.

One of Grissom's classic all-time screw ups involved a boating accident where two persons were decapitated down along the Inter-Coastal Canal in Brazoria County. Fred Gibbs and his white trash fishing buddy Mike Newlish had been drinking all day when they came flying down the Inter-Coastal near Sergeant, Texas. Both men were standing up when they came off the bay and went under the drawbridge. They had been through there a hundred times and knew better. They were also feeling no pain according to their blood-alcohol levels at the time of autopsy. The cable that was stretched about five feet above the high water mark cut like a knife when they hit it running thirty-five miles per hour. Both bodies and heads were recovered and packed off to the medical examiner's office in Galveston County. The drawbridge operator was also very much worse for the wear and stayed drunk for two days before returning to work. The bodies were identified by fingerprints and toe tags designated one from the next. Figuring out whose head was whose was done from the driver's license photos.

The families of both Fred Gibbs and Mike Newlish lived in close proximity to the Grissom Funeral Home. Neither family had done business with the company since the elder Grissom turned over the reins of the business to Steve. Both families opted to use the neighborhood funeral home that their families had used as long as any of them could remember. The Newlish family decided to have Michael cremated and they planned to sprinkle his ashes off the stern of the Bolivar Ferry someday. Fred Gibbs' family wanted a standard funeral service in the funeral home chapel followed by a burial service at the Veteran's Cemetery. There was no viewing of the body the night before the services and the first anyone saw of Uncle Fred post mortem was at the funeral service.

Unfortunately Steve Grissom's haphazard organization mixed up the heads between the two bodies. Fred Gibbs' body was sporting Mike Newlish's low-rent head when people came into the service to pay their last respects. Nobody in the family liked Mike Newlish in the first place. They had never really understand why Uncle Fred ran around with that sorry no-good individual in the first place. To make matters worse Mike Newlish's remains had been cremated the day before Fred Gibbs' funeral. The police had to be called to the funeral parlor to subdue the uproar from the family that followed the mix-up. After the fact, Fred's son stated that his father hated funerals and would have enjoyed the fact that his send-off had been a less than somber affair. The final result of the day was that Big Fred and his buddy's head went into the ground following a memorial service where the casket was not even in the room.

There are many stories in the big city—and fortunately for the rest of the world there are very few funeral directors like Steve Grissom. However, without guys like him around life sure would be a lot less entertaining.

SEVENTEEN

....

HE GOT CANNED

Peter Phan owned and operated a convenience store at the intersection of Lorraine and West streets in Northeast Houston. His store was a clean and well-lighted place in a neighborhood that really could not appreciate such a novel concept. Peter opened his establishment to the public every morning at seven and closed at nine every night. He arrived early and stocked the shelves. All the items displayed were either in lots of either five or ten. Mr. Phan was compulsive in his wanting everything orderly and it looked like he used a ruler to make sure everything was evenly spaced and separated on the shelves throughout the store. It was a Wednesday morning that his battered remains were found on the floor of his establishment. He had sustained a multitude of injuries to his face and head. His facial features were actually obliterated to such a degree that a positive identification of him had to be made through fingerprints and dental records. His first legitimate customer of the day walked in and found him on the floor behind the checkout counter. Blood was splattered as high as four feet above the floor level. It was obvious that the attack site was behind the counter where he was found.

An ambulance hauled the victim to LBJ County Hospital. One police unit held the scene while another checked on him at the hospital. The doctors at LBJ advised the patrol unit that Mr. Phan's survival would require divine intervention as there was really nothing they could do for him. The on-scene unit called Homicide to advise them of the situation. The two-day shift homicide lieutenants typically spent most of their time involved in petty rivalries rather than administration of duties. Their troops laughingly would tell you that both men had risen above something. One had risen far above his level of competence while the other man may have only risen above the level of a bar stool.

Whichever of these mental midgets that was duty lieutenant that day decided patrol needed to make the scene rather than bother Homicide. A crime scene unit made the scene and the primary uniformed scene officer had the presence of mind to call the Robbery division at the North Command Station. Robbery sent a pair out to make the scene, one of which was a country boy type detective called Bubba. This man lived to track down predators. Bubba said that getting to stick a .45 in some asshole's face and scream "Freeze mother**ker or I'll kill you" was better than sex. Sometimes he would clarify that he was talking about the sex he'd had with either one of his first two wives.

Bubba walked around the store and noted first that the security camera was not working. Secondly he determined that there were only two items missing from any of the super orderly store shelves. The first was one can of Ranch Style Beans that was not in place. The second was the contents of the case register. The can of beans was found behind the counter and it had in fact been the weapon of choice used to batter the poor Vietnamese shopkeeper to a pulp. The can in question was badly dented on both ends. In fact it looked like someone had attempted to open it by stomping first one end of it and then the other. The crime scene unit called for a backup because he knew the victim was going to die and he needed to get the blood spatter documented as to angle and direction. A one-man band couldn't pull it off. Ultimately the first crime scene officers were able to locate and lift the suspect's fingerprints by using macrophotography. They were bloody images that used the victim's blood for transfer the identifying images like ink.

Bubba stood around for a while and then went outside to chew some Levi Garrett and ponder on how he could identify and arrest "Ant Knee." Bubba had the hab-

it of hanging a name on everybody. He called all unidentified black male suspects Ant Knee. As he walked out of
the front door (the plow jockey turned Detective) noticed blood drops leading out of the front door and
though the parking lot.

Ant Knee had beaten Hop Sing so badly that he himself had been covered with blood. Enough so that both
the sleeves of Ant Knee's flannel shirt were completely
soaked with the "Ornamental's" blood. Bubba tracked
Ant Knee for two blocks and across a vacant lot. When
he got to the far side of the vacant lot he lost the blood
trail. He then began casting around looking to pick up
some blood sign and he found a rather large smear on
the door frame of an old weathered frame house. This
blood smear stood out—in the words of our down-home
investigator—"Like a flashing neon star on a goat's butt."

After at least three minutes of pounding on the door
of the paintless frame house, a black female answered it.
She was asked if she was all right because there had
been an attack in the area. She seemed a bit bewildered
and said she was fine. When she was asked if there was
anyone else in the house, she said her boyfriend was
asleep inside. Bubba asked her if he had been inside
with her all night and she said she did not know. She
said she had taken a sleeping pill and someone could
have brought in a brass band in and she would not have
known it. Home Girl said that her boyfriend did not live

there, but had just spent the night there last night. She signed a consent-to-search form for the cops to search her residence. Bubba and a uniformed officer rousted lover boy from his slumber. He had taken a shower, but there was still blood under each of his fingernails. A search of the house found a garbage sack in the utility room which contained Ant Knee's bloody clothes. Peter Phan's blood was also found on both a paper sack and upon money found stashed in the top of a closet.

Ant Knee was transported to the North Command Station and he gave a self-serving confession claiming that Phan was a punk (homosexual) and that he propositioned Ant Knee. The suspect said he had gotten mad and "only meant to kick the Chinaman's ass." He claimed he did not attack the man in the course of a robbery, but that stealing his money was strictly an afterthought.

The Harris County Medical Examiner's Office would document 117 separate strikes marks (locations) with a semicircular pattern (bean can impression) on the victim's head. Bubba would later quip that Ant Knee in his own defense should have claimed that he only hit the store owner twice on his own accord. Then the sear on the bean can broke and the ranch style bean can went full automatic. Then it could have become a civil liability or product liability question rather than a criminal offense situation.

In Houston (Harris County), Texas there are so many capital murder or death penalty cases that the county cannot afford to prosecute them all. It costs in excess of a million in taxpayer dollars from the initial charging of a suspect to the final execution of the sentence when the state gives a mad dog a lethal injection. The district attorney's office gets together monthly to review the capital murder charges that have been filed. They will prosecute all cases as capitals when a policeman or fireman is killed in the line of duty. People with political influence are included in the high priority as are the killings of young children. If your case is not classed as one of the above, then the rule of seven determines which cases are prosecuted as death penalty cases.

The so-called rule of seven is quietly used. The district attorney's office takes all of the capital cases that have been filed and lumps them into groups of seven. Then that group is reviewed and the most heinous case from that block of seven which has the best evidence is tried as a capital. The rest of the cases are allowed to plead to life sentences or are reduced to lesser included offenses like murder or maybe aggravated robbery. At that point you tell the family that the grand jury for some reason chose to indict the suspect on a lesser charge. There is nobody for family members to call because a grand jury system has no appeals process. A grand jury is just a group of citizens and they had already disbanded by the time the case comes up for trial anyway.

Ant Knee's killing of the store owner was exceptionally brutal, but for some reason another case in his batch of seven was deemed more important. Peter Phan's murder case lost out. Ant Knee got to plead out to life in prison for regular old murder with no affirmative finding of a deadly weapon. Without that stipulation the killer's parole would come sooner for this clearly vicious individual. Bubba would never again eat the particular brand of ranch style beans that had been used to kill the store owner. Up until the day of Mister Phan's murder they had been his favorite companion food to eat along with his barbequed brisket or ribs.

EIGHTEEN

....

CLEANING UP HIS ACT

Southwest Dispatcher: 1745 Hours—Any 20 District Unit clear and close to Twenty Edward Thirty's beat—See the complainant at XXX Western about a possible unknown DOA male in her kitchen.

The call for service came from a very hysterical woman. She was in her car a half block from her home. She'd just come in from work and found what appeared to be a dead man in her kitchen. No she had not touched him. When she saw him lying on his back, slack-jawed and with his eyes wide open she just figured he was dead. No, she did not know who he was or what he was doing in her house. "Just send me some cops, damn it!" she demanded of the dispatcher. The dispatcher finally sent the blue suits. What they found was, in fact, a very dead burglar. He had what appeared to be a small caliber bullet wound in his belly. Just who had shot him was the question they could not immediately answer. The house in question had obviously been burglarized and forced entry had been made through the back door. The home had been ransacked and some property was stacked up by the back door. It appeared the suspect or suspects had planned to carry the loot off prior to the demise of the unknown eighteen- to twenty-year-old male that lay dead in the kitchen.

This was the type of neighborhood that burglars love. The house in question was a two-story brick tract house in a subdivision where everybody has 2.2 kids and owns 2.2 cars. Most every resident in this neighborhood was mortgaged to the hilt and both spouses worked. If they don't they will lose everything they own within sixty days. Everybody has a big screen TV and a few pieces of jewelry. Some folks have a gun or two either in the bedside nightstand or in the master bedroom closet. Guns sell well on the street or they can be used as trade items at dope houses.

The patrol officers found the dead man to be in an advanced state of rigor, indicating he had been dead for several hours. To compound the strange side of this investigation was the position the body was found in. The dead man was found lying on his back. But the odd thing was that the kitchen's dishwasher was standing open with its door extended all of the way down. The body was lying on top of the open door with the dead man's head hanging back almost at a 90 degree angle to the line of the torso. His legs were straight out and his heels were touching the floor. In accordance with their training the patrol officers searched the house and secured the scene. Then they called both the Homicide duty lieutenant and the medical examiner's office. The duty lieutenant asked the first unit on the scene if they had called for an ambulance and he was told that there was no need, life had ended for this man several hours prior to their arrival.

Harmon and Forrest were assigned to make the scene by the Homicide Division's duty lieutenant. They drove to the scene and met with the homeowner, a crime scene unit and an investigator from the medical examiner's office. They noted the home had been obviously burglarized, the bedrooms ransacked, and the items stacked up near the rear entry door (which had also been the point of entry). The dead man had a wallet on his person with a valid Louisiana driver's license in the name of an eighteen-year-old named Xavier Clements. His pockets also yielded several items of interest. Therein were found one crack pipe, three pieces of jewelry identified by the homeowner as hers, as well as three one hundred dollar bills and one rock of cocaine in a small plastic bag. The homeowner, when asked if there had been any cash in the house, said she had hidden three one hundred dollar bills in the bottom of her jewelry box, and that the rings and bracelet she'd identified as being hers had been in that same box.

The dead man's name was run on the HPD computer and his name showed up on multiple occasions on the suspect screen. Under each listing the address of XXXXX Warner always appeared. After clearing the scene Harmon and Forrest grabbed a two-man uniformed unit and drove to the dead man's home address which was about three miles from the death scene and one mile from the high school he was supposed to attend. The suspect's mother was at first hostile when asked if Xavier "X" Clements lived there. When she was shown his driver's license she made a positive identification of it as being her son. This was before she was advised of his death. Lori Clements told the investigators that her son had left the house at 7:45 that morning with a friend of his named Roland "Rolo" Trimble. They were supposed to be headed to Madison High School where they were both students. The detectives ran Rolo's name and got a nearby address.

Armed with a description of Roland Trimble they drove to his address. When Harmon and Forrest got there they found X's bright-skinned and dyed orange haired good buddy sitting in a car on the street in front of his house. Unfortunately for Rolo that car was stolen. When searched, Trimble had a pair of tickets to a Rockets basketball game in his front shirt pocket. He claimed to have bought the tickets earlier in the day from a guy on the streets. Due to his possession of a stolen car, Roland Trimble got a trip to the Central police station so he could visit at length with the two investigators.

When they arrived at Homicide there was a message waiting on the detectives from a dayshift patrol officer named Troy Sikes. That officer had seen the six o'clock news and had watched the story about the dead burglar being found in the house. Sikes advised that he'd made a burglary in progress call earlier that day where a homeowner had shot at two burglars with a .22 pistol. The crooks were inside her house at the time, but they had escaped and were thought to have been uninjured. That call was only two blocks from where the dead man had been found.

It appeared that things were coming together and the investigators now had even more questions for Rolo the hot car driver. Before they went into the interview room Forrest called the homeowner where the body of Xavier Clements had been found. She advised him that yes, in fact she had determined that some Rockets basketball tickets were missing. It seemed that she and her husband had season tickets and reserved seats. She was able to give Forrest the seat numbers, which in fact matched those on the tickets that had come out of Roland Trimble's pocket. The clot was thickening, as they say in Homicide.

When confronted with the facts Roland Trimble started telling the truth about what happened that day. He and Xavier Clements had decided that instead of going to school they should do some south Harris County burglaries and get high. He claimed X had a couple of dime rocks and they smoked one each as they drove around looking for a place to break into. They found a likely looking place with two days of newspapers in the driveway as their first felony burglary site. After ringing the doorbell a couple of times they kicked in the front door. Their goal was to find stuff that they could fence or trade for more dope. Unfortunately for them that house was occupied by a woman named Deloris Torres. She had been down with the flu for two days and had been in the back bedroom when she heard her door being kicked in. Mrs. Torres called 911 and then got her husband's .22 pistol from the top shelf of his closet. She chose to make a preemptive strike as the suspects came down the hallway toward the master bedroom. Rolo advised that the woman just appeared in the doorway at the end of the hall and she began cranking off rounds at them. The suspects were thought to have fled on foot. When the police arrived the crooks were nowhere to be found. No car was seen and the Mrs. Torres could not give any sort of description other than the suspects were most likely black males.

What had in fact occurred was that Rolo and Xavier had jumped into their stolen car (Trimble claimed X had stolen it from a grocery store parking lot when they opted not to go to class). Xavier Clements was no longer available to deny or refute any of the allegations. Though Rolo put the theft on his dead buddy, he admitted possession of the stolen car, thus nailing himself on a felony *unauthorized use of a motor vehicle* charge. Rolo and X had, in fact, gone a couple of streets over and found another place that looked inviting to burglarize. X must have been so screwed up that he was feeling no pain and did not know he was gut shot. The two scholars kicked in the back door and began to ransack the house. In the master bedroom Rolo snagged a couple of Rockets tickets and a .38 revolver, while X found several pieces of jewelry and some cash in a jewelry box.

Rolo went on to say that X said that there was something felt wrong with his stomach while they were upstairs. Clements told his buddy that he'd skipped breakfast and thought he would get something to get eat in the kitchen. He went into the kitchen and heated up some sausage and a roll while he continued to search for valuables. Kitchens are often searched by burglars because sometimes people hide their valuables in the freezer or the dishwasher. Rolo said that Xavier took one bite of the sausage and then fell back onto the open dishwasher door. Clements said he though X was playing at first and after a bit he checked his buddy and determined he was not breathing. The burglar had been dead on his feet and didn't know it. When Trimble figured out that his friend was as dead as good intentions he left for parts unknown.

The two detectives got a good laugh about the possibility that the dead man's last deed was an attempt to clean up his act, but in a dishwasher. Forrest worked the scene portion of the investigation and had taken custody of the stolen jewelry, cash, the glass crack pipe and rock of cocaine that had been in X's pockets. The day following the scene investigation Clements' father called demanding the valuables that had been on his son's body. Forrest refused to release the valuables or the crack pipe and dope. The elder Clements said that if the cops thought that his son had stolen money and jewelry from the homeowners, then he must have stolen the dope and crack pipe from them too. He told Forrest that they should then file on the homeowners for possession of narcotics. The dead man's father was advised that nothing was going to be released to anyone until there was a grand jury ruling as to death of Xavier Clements. Forrest had only met the dead suspect after he assumed room temperature. However he now understood where he got his anti-social ways—from both sides of his loving family.

A grand jury from the 338th District Court cleared Deloris Torres of any criminal wrongdoing. X's death was ruled a justifiable homicide. Forrest went to the court of authority and obtained a court order to return the stolen property to its rightful owner. That left the belligerent father without further recourse and the detectives had done an effective end run around a potential Internal Affairs complaint.

The final ruling in this matter was that Xavier Clements finally cleaned up his act, and Deloris Torres had her pistol returned to her. Harmon donated a box of hyper velocity high speed .22 hollow-point bullets to Mrs. Torres.

NINETEEN

....

HELL NO!

Oliver (alias Ollie) King was a rarity. He was both wealthy and a cop. He'd reached the rank of detective/sergeant before he got into the alarm business. The business flourished and Ollie was able to enjoy the good life. Though he had well over twenty years on the department he simply would not retire. There was much speculation as to why, but nobody knew for sure. King drove a classy car and was very well dressed. His lieutenant claimed that Ollie was always dressed sharper than a country clap doctor or maybe looked like some high-rolling rubber salesman. Either way the general consensus was that he would never be identified as a cop in public. Brother King had it all, money, clothes, cars, and then he decided to pick up another accouterment of the rich and famous—a mistress.

It was a spring afternoon when Ollie came very close to being killed while on duty. He and his girlfriend had just enjoyed an early lunch at a five-star restaurant near the intersection of Louisiana and Stuart. Fifteen seconds after they exited the front door arm in arm, they were confronted by King's irate wife Doris. She screamed out rude things about Ollie's relationship with his mother before she pulled one of his own pistols out of her purse. Wifey then proceeded to shoot her beloved husband one time in the abdomen. Doris King then began to cry. Ollie's girlfriend pissed all over herself and things continued to go downhill from there. The doorman at the restaurant knew King was a cop—so he placed the emergency officer down call. Ollie got carted off to an emergency room while his wife, his girlfriend and another unlikely witness were all hauled down to the Homicide Division. Doris King had been so mad at her husband that she couldn't drive to the restaurant rendezvous site. She had enlisted her mother to drive her to what would become the shooting scene. Mommy Dearest became as startled a witness as the bleached blonde fender lizard of a girlfriend that Ollie was trying to impress.

Oliver King was lucky. His wife had picked up an old .38 Smith & Wesson caliber snub-nosed pistol he had in a desk drawer at their business office. The .38 Smith & Wesson cartridge with its round nosed lead bullet is even more under-powered than the standard .38 special. The bullet that hit Romeo (though it hurt like bloody hell) luckily did not hit any vital organs. The fired bullet traveled from front to back and came to rest under the skin on Lover Boy's right back. With only a small incision by an emergency room doctor, the spent bullet popped right out and was in good enough condition to have been reloaded into another cartridge casing and fired again.

Oliver was still in the emergency room when he was interviewed by an old Homicide investigator that got straight to the point. "Ollie, the Doctor here says it looks like you're lucky as hell and are gonna pull through all right. You know it was your wife that shot you out there today don't you?" King answered flatly, "Yeah." Then Ollie was asked if he wanted to file charges on her for the shooting. He piped up right quick saying, "Hell no, I don't! That would really piss her off!" Mrs. King was released from custody because under the state law at the time she could not be prosecuted unless the victim wanted to do so.

Ollie King went back to work in about three weeks' time. In another week after his returned to duty, his .38 Smith & Wesson revolver and the fired bullet that had been removed from his back were returned to him. King had the bullet gold plated and he wore it on a chain around his neck. The pistol that he had been shot with he had framed in a memory box and put behind glass. The framed gun had some roommates inside the memory box. They consisted of newspaper clippings from both the Houston Post and the Houston Chronicle as well as the live and fired cartridge casings that had been inside the old pistol. The cartridges were displayed with the primers facing toward the glass in the pattern they had been inside the revolver. The fired casing was up top like it had just gone off. These mementos stayed on the wall of his cubical the rest of the time he worked for the police department. He stayed with the department for a couple of more years before he retired. It is unknown however if he remained married to the same woman that ventilated him. She had not been his first wife, but she damned near was his last.

TWENTY

....

HIT MEN

Murder for hire gets a lot of attention on television and in the movies but there are actually very few professional hits. Killings within the drug trade are common, but it is both cultural and simply a part of doing business in that line of work. A lot of people may claim to have done hits or know someone who will do contract killings. In all honesty such people are thankfully very few and far between in the real world. In fact, many of the people who have actually agreed to and actually completed a murder-for-hire get stiffed or only get a small portion of the money that they were promised. Yearly there are multiple defendants arrested after they put out the word they are looking for a hit man. Instead they are put in touch with their local or state law enforcement authorities who are more than willing to help them into prison. Their motives are generally related to divorce, the killing a spouse's lover, money—or a combination of all of the above.

William Albright was murdered by a pair of killers that were nineteen and twenty years old. They were both from Arkansas and were dyed-in-the-wool white trash. They'd come to Houston with a longtime friend named Buddy Wheeler. Buddy came to the big city to make a pay check that was higher than minimum wage. His companions had nothing better to do than just to tag along. Wheeler's school chums were named Dean Montgomery and Chester Long. Upon arrival in Houston the trio stayed with a down and out cousin of Buddy Wheeler's. Buddy immediately got a construction job pouring and finishing concrete. He worked six or seven days a week, while Long and Montgomery worked odd jobs that were enough to keep them in beer and cigarette money.

William Albright was married to a barfly named Ronnie Sue. She bore him a worthless namesake of a son named Billy who, at age eighteen, neither wanted to work or to go to school. Billy and his mom were playmates while dad worked twelve- and sixteen-hour-days offshore.

Dear old dad worked ten days on and five days off. He was getting tired of supporting two lounge lizards and told Junior to go get a job or go into the military and grow up. He also told his beloved wife she could either dry out on her own or to go to Alcoholics Anonymous. She was further advised that if she did not

124

choose one or the other her next step was to pack her stuff and not let the door hit her on the ass on her way out. Mom and Junior had the sinking feeling that their gravy train was about to come to an end. They took stock of dad's estate and pension situation. The killing of William Albright would pay off his house and his loving family could then dispose of his inherited 100-acre family farm in east Texas. If he died, then Ronnie Sue would get half of William's pension for life or until such time as she was to remarry. If Ronnie's better half kicked her out she and Billy might have to get jobs and worse yet might have to take on adult responsibilities.

Mom and Junior met the Arkansas inbreds Dean Montgomery and Chester Long at the Cedars Lounge off the Eastex Freeway on Houston's far north side. All four of the individuals in question could have been related. They began to hang out together and a plot was hatched for the inbreds to kill the elder William Albright. The baptized-in-beer quartet settled on a five thousand dollar price tag for the capital murder. Montgomery and Long didn't want to act like country bumpkins now that they'd agreed to do their first contract killing. As such, the four lame-brains sat down at the Albright kitchen table and drafted a document. It stipulated the cost and promised payment program for the proposed killing of the only worthwhile member of the Albright family. Then they all signed and dated the document to make it official. The two wanna-be hit men kept the contract with them to properly ensure payment at a later date. The two killers (in the making) even discussed their planned job with Buddy Wheeler. Wheeler told them they were full of crap and if they wanted money they could come work twelve hour days in the summer sun with him. He would later tell the police that they talked about their big pending job—but he really never took them seriously.

Buddy worked and paid weekly rent for room and board to his cousin. Montgomery and Long sometimes slept on the floor in Buddy's room and they did not have kitchen privileges after their first week in Houston. On the night of August 3rd at nine thirty at night Montgomery and Long woke Buddy Wheeler up and told them they needed a ride to the Albright family home. They had Buddy park around the corner from Ronnie Sue and Billy's house while they ran inside for a few minutes. They said that Ronnie Sue had called and said Billy was on a date. She'd supposedly told them that if they'd come by right now she would screw the both of them. Buddy was so tired he fell asleep waiting for his friends to return. They awoke him in a bit and told him to drive back home. He did so and fell back asleep as soon as his head hit the pillow.

The next day when the home invasion and murder of William Albright hit the news, the phones in Homicide started ringing. The stupid twins had talked their business up at more than one beer joint. Neither defendant owned a car, but their roommate Buddy Wheeler did. Montgomery had two misdemeanor hot check warrants out of Hot Springs. He and Long were drinking in a north side beer joint when the Homicide detectives found them. The police offense report indicated that Long "volunteered" to go with the investigators along with his friend Montgomery. They were reported to say that they had nothing to hide. Buddy Wheeler was picked up from his job. He could not have been more helpful. Wheeler got lucky because he got interviewed by two detectives named Forrest and Harmon. Buddy was terribly upset that the two slugs he had grown up with done such a thing. He told the detectives that his friends had talked about killing Mister Albright for insurance money and his estate. He also thought in all honesty they were just strutting around trying to act like a couple of tough guys. Buddy then began blaming himself. "I'm every bit as guilty of this killing as they are," he proclaimed. "I heard those two talking about doing a contract killing, and they got me up to drive them to and from the Albright's home last night."

Buddy was steered away from his guilt trip by the two older detectives. The detectives knew they needed a credible witness who had no criminal history and who was reputably employed. Their star witness also dropped the cases best evidence yet in their laps. Wheeler knew about the fact that Mommy Dearest and her loving son Billy, along with the dumbass killers had put the details on paper—an actual contract killing. Harmon and Forrest were told that the Arkansas mullets didn't altogether trust the Albrights, so they got them to spell out their promise of five thousand dollars in exchange for the murder of William Albright. Then they all four signed and dated the document. To make matters even better the killers stored this document in Wheeler's bedroom for safe keeping. A warrant produced the only known written details and stipulations of a "contract" killing that the two detectives had ever seen.

The investigation ultimately ended in four life sentences. None of the idiots involved in this matter had much of a criminal history. It would be difficult to prove to a jury beyond a reasonable doubt that the four defendants would be an ongoing threat to society if they were ever released from prison. Due to that fact the state did not seek the death penalty. All four of the suspects in this case were tried and convicted of capital murder. They are all currently serving life sentences in the Texas Department of Criminal Justice. Stupid is as stupid does.

TWENTY-ONE

....

ANGOLA PRISON

Much of the state of Texas looks upon the state of Louisiana as a third world country. Those that have spent much time in their (Louisiana's) legal and criminal justice system will often agree. Things just happen in Louisiana. A Houston Homicide detective named Mike Striker had a murder case where an Asian male was killed in his home. The dead man's wallet and car were both stolen. The only possible lead in the case was that the next day a mixed blood Asian was reportedly seen driving a car very similar to the one that had been stolen. That possible suspect was known by name and said to have a bad reputation in the Vietnamese community. He was half-Vietnamese and half-black and was said to be from a coastal town in Louisiana. There had been no positive identification of the car he'd been driving, like a license plate or by some identifying characteristics. It was simply a matter of his being seen driving a car similar to the dead man's on the day after the murder. In fact the murder had not yet been discovered when he was observed driving around in southwest Houston.

The car was the only lead in the case. The fingerprints lifted at the scene were only those of the victim and from some unidentified person. The named person (Nia Van Tran) who had been seen in a car similar to the one that was missing had no fingerprints on file in either Houston or Louisiana. In fact he had been an adult only six months at the time of the murder. Tran was supposed to be a deck hand working on a boat called the Lady D that was doing bay shrimping out of Cameron Parish, Louisiana. The murder victim's car did not surface for two months. It had been found abandoned in a roadside park by a deputy sheriff just inside of Cameron, Louisiana.

That deputy had stopped on the highway and written tickets to three Asian males for hitchhiking just prior to finding the car. It turned out Nia Van Tran was one of the three people issued tickets for that minor infraction. The vehicle's license plates had been removed. The car had a Texas inspection sticker, but the County Mounty wrote the VIN number down wrong (he transposed two numbers) so the car did not come back stolen when he checked it. The abandoned car was towed to a wrecker storage lot. Only when it came up for auction at a state salvage sale only then was it determined to have been stolen in a capital murder.

Mike Striker called the deputy that recovered the vehicle. When he found out about the tickets and determined Nia Van Tran had been located near the scene he was elated. The wanted vehicle would basically not be worth much in the way of evidence. It had been rummaged through a couple of times by storage lot employees looking for anything of value and the heat and humidity would have destroyed any prints that had been left behind.

Mike actually called to see if Tran was known to the sheriff's department by name or reputation and to see if the suspect had any local open warrants. Mike was told "Just let me know when you want to come and interview him and I will have him waiting for you in our parish prison." The detective explained to the deputy that he did not have enough probable cause to get a warrant for the suspect's arrest. The deputy simply laughed and said, "Don't you worry about that Bud. You see, everything is illegal down here in Louisiana." Tran had an open warrant for his hitchhiking ticket and the high sheriff contacted the Coast Guard and had one of their patrol boats locate the Lady D and arrest the capital murder suspect for the hitchhiking warrant. When that Houston sergeant arrived in the southern coastal parish later that afternoon the suspect was in a cell and waiting on him. The suspect confessed.

This story has not been written to slight the men and women in law enforcement in Louisiana. They will never fail to assist another agency to the maximum degree when requested. They are always invaluable as they can guide the out-of-state officers through their local rules and procedures. It also never hurts if you buy the locals a couple of cold beers when they go off duty as a friendly gesture. In New Orleans you may not have to wait until the end of their shift. There is an old joke is that in some jurisdictions that you can get fired for drinking beer on duty. In New Orleans it is said that you can get fired for *not* drinking beer on duty.

Angola prison is Louisiana's high security penal operation that is an eighteen hundred-acre working prison farm as well. The Mississippi river borders the property on three sides and the best access to it is by motor launch rather than attempting to get there by roadway. Convict labor first appeared on the Angola when Samuel James bought and merged several plantations back in 1860. He then leased convict laborers from the state in order to work his land. At that time it was a common practice throughout the Deep South that the state would rent out its prisoners as laborers. The land owners provided bunk houses and cook shacks and the states billed them by the day for each convict laborer. In 1901 the state of Louisiana bought the plantation and took complete control of the land and its operation. In 1916 in an attempt to save money the state fired all the prison guards and put armed trustees in charge of the prison. The end result was said to have been bedlam.

The prison system in question has vastly improved but discipline and hard work has always been the first order of the day. Angola prison is run under two concepts. The first is "You have to keep the inmates working all day so they are tired at night." The second is, "Many of these men have never done anything constructive in their lives. Now they will be able to look back upon the fruits of their labor and say *my, that certainly is a finely hoed row of corn!*" If you should step out of line you will be straightened out in short order. In the year 2001, a group known as The Angola 3 were let out of solitary confinement. Two of the men had been there for thirty-five years while the other man had been so housed for a mere thirty years. The concept of cruel and unusual punishment being unlawful does not seem to exist in Louisiana.

The inmates in Angola Prison should never be confused with a group of psalm singers and Sunday school teachers. Their crimes are far worse than that of breaking wind in public. They would not be there if they had not been deemed to be violent and a bona fide threat to society. It is not a pleasant place to live and work and was not designed to be. The inmate population lives and works in a hot and swampy place where everything mildews. The convicts in this prison are all serving very long sentences. They have been deemed the baddest of the bad. Only one out of six persons sent there will ever live long enough to walk out of the prison gates at the end of their incarceration period.

Police investigators everywhere have to go into prisons on a regular basis to interview inmates. They do so because prisoners have information on crimes and were either witnesses or suspects in yet other cases prior to their being sent up the river. Detectives from Texas report encountering the same unusual phenomenon when interviewing convicts inside Angola Prison. The convicts there are cooperative and whenever possible they truly want to confess to committing some crime in Texas. If they can not do that they are willing to admit to being a witness to some crime that was committed in Texas. Their goal is two pronged. If charged in Texas with a crime they will be writted back to Texas by a court order. They will then be housed in a county jail—hopefully one with air conditioning. The real hope of the Angola inmate is that he can be convicted of a felony charge in Texas and get sentenced to prison time there. That way he can serve his penitentiary time in Texas and get credit in Louisiana for time served, but in a nicer facility. Louisiana will gladly let Texas pay to incarcerate their prisoners for them while they serve out their Texas prison sentences.

Prisons are like small towns. Convicts that can type and do clerical tasks are used in administrative office positions. They are thrilled to do so because they get to work in an air-conditioned environment. As such they are always ultra-polite and can never do enough to help out. They also see all the correspondence and glean every bit of information about everything they can about what is going on in their prison world. The cons know when detectives from Texas are coming in and who they are going to interview. The word spreads through the population of the prison about where the investigators are coming from. By the time the cops get to Angola (no small task in itself) the prison chaplain already has a list of names he will pass along to the investigators. That list will contain the names of inmates who want to speak to them about crimes committed in their jurisdiction. Those convicts are more than willing to openly confess to crimes they either committed or witnessed in Texas. Truth is always stranger than fiction and the Angola inmates are always hopeful that the truth might set them free. Free from that particular Louisiana penal institution, at least for a while.

TWENTY-TWO

....

Q-PATROL

With the coming of political correctness and a more progressive (translates to liberal) orientation in the nation's 4th largest city's government, the gay community got the ear of Houston's City Hall. The flaming members of that community have long been a point of interest with Houston's suburban high school kids. On weekends the teenagers and young adults from the suburbs will often come into the Montrose area of Houston to gawk at the Gay Blades as they strut their stuff. Friday and Saturday nights are prime time viewing hours when coming into town to view the freak show put on by the trolling and strolling members of the indefinite sex. Departmental in-service training sessions often would advise almost every other year that offense reports should not be titled Rolling of a Queer, but that Robbery by Assault was in fact the correct offense report title. Assaults upon the sissy-guys were often perpetuated by street people and sometimes by groups of young rednecks or suburban high school jocks.

Following one attack that turned into a homicide and a double aggravated assault stabbing, the heat was turned up on the police department to do something to stop such activities. Up until that point nobody had gotten too excited about a few faggots getting their butts kicked. The practice of rolling queers had been going on for generations. Now the term hate crime began being bandied about and sexual orientation became as important as race when determining victim status. A whole new group of victims was born and politicians were going to make hay while the sun was shining.

The police department was told by the mayor that it was time to make a public showing that the attacks upon the limp wrested population were no longer to be tolerated. First a full court press was made to arrest the killer of the now sainted Gay Blade. Following the arrest of three murder suspects in their early twenties the police decided to make a public showing of arresting persons out to beat up or robbing homosexuals. The decision was made to put plainclothes street officers out as decoys in an attempt to get the trashy element to attempt to rob or assault them. That way the city council, mayor and police could be seen as caring and proactive with regard to crimes against fruitcakes. If the program blew up the city officials would simply blame everything on the cops and step back from the mess and claim no association with it.

When officers out of the Central station were polled, several volunteered for the decoy duty. They, along with some of the district supervisors met with some gay community leaders who heralded the idea. Then the gays wanted to assist the cops by telling them the areas they'd heard were spots where attacks upon the sweet guys were taking place. The street cops were really taken back when the gays began telling them how to dress and act so that they would better blend in with the gays on the street. One street sergeant commented after the first meeting "I thought for a minute some of those fruitcakes we were forced to meet with were going to give us tips on how to do our hair and the proper application of makeup. I thought I was going to puke."

It did not take too long before a group of rednecks decided to confront the plainclothes officers. The twenty-two to twenty-five-year old white trash types in a pickup pulled up and asked the cops, "Are you guys gay?" When the rednecks got an affirmative answer all three of the truck's passengers bailed out. Two of the gentlemen brandished baseball bats and the driver had a tire tool in his hand. The cops pulled out their off-duty pistols and identified themselves as police. The two men carrying the bats dropped their weapons immediately. The truck's driver shouted out "That's Bull-----! You guys ain't cops. This is Houston where all the cops carry big damned guns and shoot the hell out of people!" The sergeant at the scene shoved his .380 Walther into his hip pocket and pulled a stainless steel .357 with a 4-inch barrel out of his cowboy boot. Rodney Allen Redneck dropped his tire tool and meekly said, "Anything you say officer" and he put his palms against the front fender of his truck as he assumed the position.

Following a couple of such arrests the then-chief of police held a news conference where he discussed the decoy operation and the great success in arresting gay bashers. There were a couple of more sting situations set up during the following year to locate and arrest suspects targeting gay men in the lower Westheimer district. The draftees chosen for this assignment were thereafter told to report on a certain day and time for what came to be known as "Q-Patrol." To make matters worse a group of gay blades heard the name and liked it enough that they began a citizen's neighborhood patrol with walkie-talkie radios and doing both mobile and foot patrols. The new social club even began wearing t-shirts with Q PATROL stenciled across their backs. The cops dropped the term from their vocabulary immediately.

TWENTY-THREE

I KEPT HEARING HIS VOICE

The desire to get either an adrenaline rush or high, coupled with the desire not to work in a boring job, draws many young people into police work. Some want to make a difference in their world. Still others search for adventure and life in the fast lane. There are also a few folks out there that are drawn to the life strictly for a paycheck. We however don't claim persons in that category very often. No matter what caused you to come to the job, it can and will oftentimes put its mark upon you. Sometimes what you encounter in life sears deeper into your soul than most people would ever believe. With luck you will never get a chance to experience such a thing. The following is the series of events that marked several good street cops.

Juan "Tacquache" Salas was a wife-beating mucho macho east-end Houston Chicano. He was a sawed-off beer joint Super Vato with an "all the women want me" kind of attitude. Fighting was not his forte, but after two beers he turned into a little rooster that wanted to take care of every hen in the barnyard. A few years ago (on July 30th as a matter of fact) his wife Anna divorced him. She did so after bearing him two children and absorbing more than her fair share of physical abuse.

While the divorce was pending he was arrested and charged with a family violence related assault charge that took place in Anna's mother's front yard. To that charge he pled guilty and received two years of misdemeanor probation along with anger management classes. Coupling anger management classes with probated sentences has become real popular in our politically correct society. Street cops will tell you that they feel that if stupid had some of his teeth loosened and passed blood in his urine for three days he might better understand the error of his ways. What's more he might even understand what an abused wife goes through. But I digress.

It was 10 a.m. when the family law judge spelled out the terms of the divorce decree. Salas was ordered to pay half of his net income in the form of monthly child support payments. He was further mandated by the court (because of his spousal abuse conviction) not to come within 300 feet of his ex-wife or her parents' home. What is more he could only have supervised visitation of his two children, and then only at a court designated safe location. The only thing the judge did not say was "And may God have mercy upon your mortal soul."

Super Vato quietly left the courthouse a few minutes after the divorce was granted. He then drove back to his ratty garage apartment. There he drank two beers and picked up his beloved stainless steel .44-magnum Ruger Redhawk revolver. His next stop was the home of his former in-laws.

After several tries Tacquache was able to finally kick his way through the front door of the woman who had shamed him and had taken his kids from him. Though he had lost the element of surprise he was thrilled that he was terrorizing the women inside as they screamed and yelled. His former mother-in-law was able to get through to the 911 operator while stupid was making entry into the family home. The dispatcher was informed that the suspect was armed with a pistol and was threatening to kill everyone in the house. Then the phone went dead.

Former momma-in-law and ex-wife were both soundly pistol-whipped by Mister Macho before he grabbed up both of the kids and waltzed out through the shattered front door. The area patrol units knew the location of the house and the suspect because they'd had to fight and arrest him there before. They arrived in time to see Salas loading the kids into his ragged-out Chevy Astro Van. The patrol units pulled up in such a way that they blocked the van in both front and rear. The third police car pulled up and made a 45 degree angle with the cop

SGT. BRIAN FOSTER

car blocking the van's forward motion. The officer driving the car that blocked the rear of the van moved to a position behind the engine block of a parked car across the street. His goal was not to be in the line of fire of the three officers at the front of Vato's van. From this point on the whole hostage situation just kept getting worse.

The infant was strapped into a child's car seat which was lashed to the front passenger's bucket seat. Juan Salas had his horse pistol pointed at the infant's head. The blue suits had taken cover behind engine blocks and were calling out to their cornered suspect in both English and Spanish. They told him to put down the gun and they could talk the matter over. Nobody needed to get hurt they told him. Juan was in the driver's seat and his three-year-old stood on the transmission hump between the front seats. Several of the officers present said that Juan appeared to first make eye contact with them and then to nod his head. It appeared to them that he was going to give up. The cops all agreed that the suspect slowly opened the driver's door and swung his legs outside of the vehicle.

As he stepped out of the van Juan quickly grabbed his oldest child and pulled him out with him. His namesake Juanito began protesting loudly by yelling out, "No Daddy—Daddy Stop!" Juan pulled the kid around in front of him in a position between him and the cops, like you would expect someone to do when they had what is called a human shield. He pressed the muzzle of the big .44 pistol against the ribcage of his son as he pulled him close.

Everyone present was caught completely off guard when Salas fired a single round that coursed from side to side through the little boy's chest. In a single motion the psycho of the year dropped his son and spun firing at his infant's head. The .44 magnum made a *whoomp* sound inside the closed van when it extinguished the ten-month-old's life. Juan then turned with gun in hand to face the four stunned officers that were drawn into the firing squad for Juan Xavier Salas' assisted suicide. The only non-shooter was an officer named Bobby. He held his fire because another officer jumped between him and the suspect just as Salas committed Copicide.

The Psychological Services Unit chief saw the whole episode unfold live on the noon news. He rounded up the other psychologists that were at work that day and they all went directly to the scene. All of the officers present were parents and reported having nightmares from what they saw that day. None of the officers had regrets about shooting the murdering scumbag Tac-quache Salas to death. What haunted them was the "If I had only acted sooners" and the "Why didn't I realizes."

Bobby reported hearing the three-year-old cry out "No Daddy—Daddy Stop" for somewhere between two and three months. He also said that it was upwards of six months before he stopped dreaming and witnessing the murders in vivid colors. He felt this was odd because all his life he'd dreamed in black and white. Drinking helped only because hangovers kept the "What-ifs" at bay. Everybody involved in the shooting agreed that the psychological counseling helped. Not all the scars you pick up on the street can be seen from the outside.

Fifty percent of the rounds expended at Juan Salas hit their intended target, which was not bad for a police shooting. None of the misses hit the cadavers of the murdered children. This similarly was good because it kept the media from having a field day. Some news directors routinely order autopsy reports to see if they can create news by alleging what the police said and what the autopsy said were two different animals. The following situation is an example of such a situation.

A Narcotics officer once shot and killed a three-time convicted felon female junkie. The shooting occurred as she was attempting to rob him. The autopsy reported that the rounds went from back to front, thereby making the shooting rather questionable and contrary to what the officer's earlier sworn statement said. This information was also contrary to what the pathologist told the investigators at the autopsy proceedings the morning after the killing. The officer in question was relieved of duty while the investigation continued.

His name and the fact he was being investigated for the possible murder of a grandmother of three had been splattered all over the newspaper and television channels. He tried to explain to his seven-year-old daughter that he was only protecting himself from somebody who was trying to hurt him. He had been involved in a total of three shootings, and all the parties he had shot were always minority group members. To make matters worse his daughter was beaten up at school by some other school children. The morgue photos were reviewed and the autopsy findings were changed to show the true nature of the injuries. The officer in question was exonerated. None of the television stations would air a retraction. It was "old news," you see. The newspaper did print a retraction on a far back page. The medical examiner's office was blamed for inaccurately printing the actual findings of the autopsy.

Now back to the police shooting of the rehabilitated the child killer Juan Salas. An interesting aside in the Salas murder case came out in his autopsy. Salas died from multiple police gunshots. Abrasions showed he fell on his back after being shot. The unusual discovery was that Juan had several broken upper and lower front teeth. They were reportedly broken posthumously. It was speculated that someone stomped the cadaver in the face after the fact. However nobody involved in the investigation really cared one way or the other.

TWENTY-FOUR

I'LL BUY YOU BREAKFAST IF---

The night shift officers out of the Park Place Station called themselves the Park Place Rangers, after the U.S. Army Rangers. The part of Houston that they policed was rough enough during daylight hours. When the sun went down things really got rough. The area inhabitants (that worked) were generally blue collar working class folks. They tended to be plain spoken as well as rough and tumble in nature. All three ethnic groups were well represented in southeast Houston. The night shift southeast patrol troops were generally a skull-cracking and shooting lot. They got worse after a lame-brained night shift lieutenant came into roll call one night and made the statement, "Boys—in my book the only good burglar is a dead burglar." One of his sergeants complained that he had effectively opened hunting season on all burglars. There was now no closed season and no bag limit on them.

The following shooting scenario is one that nobody will ever claim responsibility for. The suspect (Ronnie Earl Wiggins) is long dead and gone. If his IQ had been two points lower he could have been justified in claiming he was a house plant. Though he could neither read nor write very well, his one life skill was that he could break and enter with the best of them. His last breaking and entering job was at an auto parts store. The business had a silent alarm. It was a slow night and several units responded to the call, though only a single two-man unit broke the air acknowledging they were in route. A total of five marked cars pulled up on the scene before Ronnie knew he was trapped. They were positioned facing each of the four corners of the building and the original unit was directly in front of the store's front doors. When the police cars all turned their headlights on at the same time Ronnie could be seen running around inside the building. He was looking for a way out that did not exist. All possible escape routes were blocked by men with guns.

The beat car never acknowledged to the dispatcher that they had a burglar in the building. That specific unit on that night was manned by two notorious street cops. Their police car was about thirty feet in front of the front doors of the business as they watched Ronnie Earl run frantically back and forth inside the building. The district police sergeant (who was a killer in his own right) pulled up at the scene. He walked up to the beat officers and told Greg Woolsey (the younger of the two cops) "I'll buy you breakfast if you can kill him from here" as the sergeant pointed at the frantic suspect. The slim blonde-headed cop drew his .44-caliber revolver and in one smooth motion came to a two-handed shooting position and center-punched Ronnie with a hand loaded 180 grain jacketed Sierra hollow-point bullet. The bullet coursed through a plate glass window prior to slamming into the suspect's torso. Ronnie was sent directly to the big jail house in the sky without passing *Go* or collecting two hundred dollars.

The other units present drove off after viewing the handiwork of one of their own. A cheap .38 revolver was found beside the body of the rehabilitated burglar when the cops entered the building. It seems the crook pointed a handgun at the two officers when he saw they'd pulled up in front of the business and illuminated him on their headlights.

Greg had been forced to defend the lives of both he and his partner that night. The dead man was found to be a parole violator and wanted in two other burglary cases. The world was now declared to be a better place by a Harris County grand jury six weeks later. Urban renewal was the unofficial ruling. The patrol district sergeant was reportedly thereafter a bit more prudent regarding his offhand comments around the troops.

Park Place Rangers—No Strangers to Danger.

TWENTY-FIVE

....

IN THE NAME OF LOVE

The killing took place in Houston's Fifth Ward in the 5300 block of Lorraine Street. It was a Sunday afternoon and 93 degrees in the shade. In the summer months crimes involving physical violence soar. Social psychologists have theories to explain the actions of the downtrodden among us. Street cops don't care why it happens, but they will tell you that when the air temperature begins creeping toward body temperature that people in low income areas get irritable and irrational. Couple low intellect and no air conditioning with people that think they can cool off by drinking a couple of beers and things can get downright explosive. Their irritation seems to be fueled by the heat and squalor they live in. In this particular instance the shooter and the shootee were both bottom-feeding slum-dwelling drug dealers.

The reason behind the urban renewal killing of Marvis Collins by Junius St. Julian was that both men lusted after the affections of the same Nubian Princess. To make the situation even odder, both of the named men had full and complete knowledge that the woman they both desired (called by the street name of Fuggie) was a full-blown carrier of the AIDS virus. At the time of his death, Marvis Collins was out on bond for the killing of another idiot called Big Willie Williams. Big Willie had ripped off Marvis for some dope and Mrs. Collin's son was duty bound to send Willie to meet his maker. It was nothing personal but was strictly a standard business practice in the illicit pharmaceutical industry. If you get ripped off you must make an example of the offending party or you will become fair game for every drug dependant illegitimate piece of trash in town.

As our drama unfolds the two bucks in full rut came upon one another on the corner of Lorraine and Sumpter. With much bravado Marvis Collins pulled his shirt off and threw it to the ground in preparation to do battle with his rival. Junius St. Julian calmly just strolled up to the soon to be late Mr. Collins and pulled a .32-caliber automatic Keltec pistol from his designer jeans hip pocket. He then used his mouse gun to stitch a straight line up Marvis' torso with jacketed Winchester brand bullets. The entry holes began at the top of Collins' pubic hair and stopped at the supra-sternal notch at the top of his breast bone. This maneuver with any sort of firearm is sometimes referred to as buttoning someone's shirt. It is a terribly effective method with most any caliber weapon. Punching multiple holes in the listed mother's son brought about the desired result and Marvis Collins passed on to his just (or unjust) rewards.

Junius St. Julian (who was known by the street name of Saint) fled the scene on foot and would turn himself into the police two hours later. This killing would pass through the annals of police investigations unnoticed had it not been for the antics of the friends and family of the dead man and a smattering of street animals in the Fifth Ward. When the first patrol units arrived at the urban blight removal OSHA murder scene (violent death to a dope dealer is an occupational safety hazard) they found paramedics already on site and pronouncing Marvis to be DRT. DRT is a police and fire department term standing for **Dead Right There**. Marvis was in all actuality DRT several times over. The blue suits called for a crime scene unit and notified Homicide of the trash killing that was cluttering up Lorraine Street. After a patrol supervisor arrived and strung up crime scene tape the uniformed officers began working the crowd in an attempt to locate any eye witnesses to the actual shooting. That was about the time an opportunist street jackal showed up. Jackals and hyenas in Africa are scavengers most of the time. They work in packs generally and if given an easy chance to kill a non-threatening prey animal they will not hesitate. The feral human street jackals usually operate in the same manner. They also exhibit a similar mind set and will prey on the weak or helpless whenever they get an opportunity.

Marvelous Marvis Collins (as he chose to bill himself in life) was in his opinion an upstanding dope dealer in the community. As such he wanted to be known by a trademark. He chose to be recognized by the snake skin boots and shoes that he always wore in public. On the day of his demise he was wearing a pair of custom made snake skin tennis shoes. His shoes were what the street trash had been trying to steal as his body lay under a sheet. Just after the first scavenger was run off by the uniformed officers the family of the newly-sainted Marvis Collins showed up. They began to wail a chorus of "Oh Laud" and "Oh Jaysus" immediately. When the family heard of some other street trash trying to steal the dead man's shoes they became quite hostile. The uniformed officers who were trying to contain the crime scene began having hostile family or supposed family members scream obscenities at them and try to storm through the crime scene tape. The street cops called for additional troops to assist with crowd control. There were a total of ten officers and a sergeant inside the crime scene tape when things really went to shit.

The friends and family of the dearly departed (he was dearly and has now departed) became really angry and decided to reclaim the body from the cops. They came through the crime scene tape and grabbed up the body and attempted to haul it off to who knows where. The cops tried to stop them and the mob began throwing punches at the cops. Out came the nightsticks and a wholesale ass-whipping began until the body was dropped and the wave of humanity moved back beyond where the crime scene tape had been. The charging of the hostile mob of lame-brains would occur first from one side of the street and then the horde on the opposite side of the street would get frenzied up enough to charge the blue suits. After the second charge of the irrational Ward Rats the cops figured out how the locals seemed to be executing their game plan. The uniformed troops would line up on the side of the body where the wild-eyed and screaming folks were as they readied themselves for the next charge.

There were a total of five charges through the police lines that day. No Philistines were arrested that day but tons of 'em were smote hip and thigh—and upside the head as well. One of the primary officers out there said it was a thing of beauty to have been part of. He would later liken it to the movie Zulu Dawn. By the time Homicide got out to the scene whatever had been there originally was well trampled and the witnesses were scattered to Hades by the riot atmosphere.

The dead man's AIDS-infected girlfriend known to one and all as Fuggie made an appearance to yell out "Junius-get up Junius" for about thirty seconds before she became overcome by emotion and passed out. In The Hood, swooning or fainting is called "falling out." The past tense of this verb is "Done fell out." Following her dying swan act Miss Fuggie was carried off by members of the onlooking crowd. Interestingly enough the now-mourning Fuggie was out of a relationship (shack job) for maybe a total of twenty-four hours. Saint Junius' killer was out on bond twelve hours after he turned himself in. Within another six to eight hours Sweet Fuggie was living the life of a dope dealer's new show pony—in the arms of Junius' killer. Nobody ever said that the life of a coin-operated machine was ever going to be easy—or even understandable—for a normal thinking person.

Author's Note: It is not possible for a normal thinking person to relate to the logic or lack thereof reported in this story. First you must understand that you live in a life-oriented world—and people in the drug culture do not. Be glad if you are not capable of grasping or understanding their thought processes. Be aware however that these folks exist and from all outward appearances cannot be distinguished from normal human beings.

TWENTY-SIX

....

JUST PISS ON 'EM

Riley Jenkins was, among other things, a contract killer. It was not a full-time job but rather a side job that paid for bad habits and such. He had been trained as a machinist following his discharge from the Marine Corps. His knowledge of the martial arts, firearms and metallurgy was extensive. At the end of a losing bout with cancer and being armed with the knowledge of his impending death he confessed his sins to a deputy named Clyde Gleason with the Montgomery County Sheriff's Department. Montgomery County lies north of the city of Houston and its county seat is Conroe. This area is where the coastal plains end and East Texas begins to rear its head. Some people hold to the adage that everything east of Interstate Highway 45 should be deeded to the state of Louisiana. That would be inclusive of Conroe and its inhabitants. Many of the local folks found living in the area could have been movie stars in the movie Deliverance. Where pine trees grow it appears that incest and inbreds go.

From his death bed, Riley confided in Clyde Gleason that he settled in Conroe, Texas under the federal Witness Protection Program. His testimony in a mid-west Mob operation got him sprung from a federal illegal weapons manufacturing charge, which in fact had been his only arrest. Jenkins settled into small town life but drifted into Houston's north side about twice a month to gamble, drink and womanize. When you are keeping a low profile you do not let your hair down too close to home. Similarly you do not have your driver's license or license plates registered to where you live. His home that the government provided was similarly not titled to him, but someone else, and all tax information was sent to a series of forwarding private post office boxes that finally routed it to his post office box in Conroe. The man could no longer go to Las Vegas, Nevada or any horse tracks for fear of being recognized by the spotters. He had broken from his old lifestyle and kept on the outskirts of a lesser fast lane.

The activities at the Vagabond Motel and nightclub just off Houston's North Freeway filled all his needs. Our boy had a shady second cousin living in Houston with whom he had been close in his youth. That party had married into a family that was in the funeral home industry. Good old cuz introduced Riley to Bob Noir.

Mister Noir controlled a huge gambling empire. His territory included northern Harris County (Houston) and all of the little towns north of Houston for about seventy-five miles on either side of Interstate 45.

One of the problems people like Bob Noir have with being the lead dog in the pack is that you have to deal with all of the mutts behind you. They at times nip at your heels and would try and pull you down and take over your position if they can. Bob Noir would at times have problems eliminated by a fellow out of Huntsville that did some collection work for him. Riley, however, came highly recommended by a gambler with 24-hour access to a crematory oven. Organized crime types like to have a connection with people who can dispose of a body without identifiable traces. You see, all DNA identifiers go away after two hours at two thousand degrees Fahrenheit. What bones are left behind then are run through a pulverizing machine. Dust to dust and ashes to ashes is always the end result.

It was a marriage made in heaven. Riley was a nondescript, clean cut and pleasant looking guy. He was also completely without morals and came equipped with blinding speed and twenty ways to kill you. His Witness Protection situation gave him a new name and identity. His middle class house was paid for and he got the standard year's worth of living expenses from Uncle Sam. With his thirty to forty hours a week job at the machine shop and his side interests with Noir (maybe nine or ten jobs a year) he enjoyed a good life while keeping his mouth shut and putting his money in a safe deposit box.

Life was not too bad. He had his job and he worked out with weights and ran daily. Twice a week he went to a martial arts studio. He studied different styles of fighting and orientations. Group lessons or working toward different colored belts was not in his game plan. Thirty minutes with an instructor was what he sought. He played poker most Wednesday nights with some neighbors and drifted into the Vagabond for the services of a knowledgeable woman two to three times a month.

When he did collections for his part-time employer a beating might simply be in order. Sometimes an example had to be made of someone that others might see. Then stolen license plates and disguises were in often used. When that sort of thing happened Bob Noir always had an airtight alibi and a herd of witnesses. If a body didn't need to be found it might simply disappear completely. It helped to have a slime ball cousin who owned a crematory oven. His cousin was not afraid of dead people, but he greatly feared Riley Jenkins. The two men had gone into the military under the buddy system and had been combat troops together. They got along— but Cousin would never cross Riley. He might shoot Riley in the back someday but he would never cross him.

The crematory manager had been more than a bit of a rough character in his youth. He also knew Riley was not quite human, but rather he was a predator of some sort that masqueraded as a human. Cousin was, however, very capable if setting his conscience aside every two to three months and do a late-night cremation for a cool thousand dollars. It was not really a bad program if you could just keep your mouth shut. Both parties concerned were raised in families where a code of silence was taught early in life.

Riley was never seen in the company of Bob Noir. They never socialized nor would they even so much as acknowledge one another if their paths crossed in a night club. When they spoke it was through someone else. The mild-mannered machinist would be contacted (usually by his cousin) and he would be given a pay phone number to call in Houston at a specific time. Riley would buy a long distance phone card and call that number from a pay phone somewhere. He would then get the information he needed. If he needed front money or an information packet with vehicle information, home address and subject information it would be provided. He was then left to his own devices. When a job was finished Cousin would send word back to the boss. Arrangements as per final payments and such were handled though a middle man. Cousin was a regular at some north side bars and he might pick up an envelope from a bartender that Noir trusted. No questions were ever asked by such people.

Riley knew the deputy (Clyde Gibson) as a customer through the specialty machine shop where he worked. Gilson was an avid collector and shooter of old Colt revolvers. Whenever Clyde needed a part made or new barrel installed he would go to the machine shop in question. The shop owner had bragged to Clyde about Riley's metal working talents. Riley's reputation was justly deserved and Jenkins liked the deputy. Gibson would ask Jenkins' opinion on possible conversions and he would pick Riley's brain about metal finishing and fabricating. The local cop could not praise the machinist's metal working abilities enough.

Our killer used several methods to ply his trade and he discussed with Clyde. His choice of weapons was both interesting and ingenious. To have a silencer in your possession was a felony in and of itself. A dryer off an automotive air conditioner system was not, however. Auto junk yards were a great source for these items and they were (and still are) available for only a few dollars.

Three or four dryers could be picked up at an auto bone yard on a single outing and gives you had a good supply. He would go to gun shows in Houston or nearby Pasadena a couple of times a year. There he would purchase one or two Ruger brand .22-caliber pistols from show patrons that were walking around carrying them.

That way there was no paper trail linking him and the weapons. The guns in question generally had heavy (sometimes called bull barrels) that are five inches in length. They are actually a target pistol but are reasonably priced. The front sights of these guns were cut off and the barrels turned to a specific diameter. Then they were threaded to a thread pattern that was compatible with that of the air conditioning dryers he obtained. A threaded cap was made to cover and protect the threads on the end of the pistol's barrel. That cap was blued with cold blue to match the gun's original finish and fit. His opinion was that if he had been caught with the gun that 99.9 percent of the cops would not know the barrel cap existed because the fit was so good and the tolerances were so close.

The automotive air conditioning dryer looks like a silencer with a tube and screw on coupler on each end. There is no barrel running through the middle of it like an actual silencer would. Riley would first cut the tube off of the end of the dryer that was not going to connect to the Ruger. Next he would shove a metal rod around .22 or .25 in diameter from the threaded end connection and through the metal packing inside the dryer. After pulling the metal rod out of the apparatus, a bullet could then be fired through it. The silencer was only good for a dozen or so shots (he told Gleason) before it no longer worked properly. The first two or three rounds were a test fire outing. The next three or so would be for the intended target. If possible Jenkins liked to shoot three rounds. Stomach, chest and head were the order he tried to place his rounds. The nose was always his intended facial shot as the bone was thinnest there and if that shot was not available he liked a base of the skull shot. He used only Remington target ammunition because it was subsonic (below 1000 feet per second) and a silencer does not work well with high speed ammunition. After a job the dryer was removed and thrown away.

Bodies that were not cremated were hauled to the national forest between Conroe and Huntsville and dragged off into the brush off some dirt road. Riley had a four-wheel-drive pickup truck with a fiberglass cap on its bed. He would put the remains in there and take them to a dump site he had scouted earlier. Following the hauling off and disposing of the remains of the dearly departed he would then go to a car wash and hose off his truck and the inside of the truck bed. The truck's bed would then be hosed down with a 50-50 solution of water and chlorine bleach he brought to the car wash with him in a pump up tank sprayer. All DNA identifiers would thereby be destroyed. Some of the persons hauled to the national forest were not dead when they got there. They might have been kidnapped and hog-tied with plastic handcuffs obtained from a police supply house. Duct tape was placed over their mouths. They were then just pulled from the truck and dispatched after they were dragged into the brush thirty or forty feet from the road.

The strangest thing about all of these killings was how Jenkins said he hastened the breakdown of the bodies so they decomposed in a matter of only a few days. He said he would expose the face of the cadaver to the elements and many times shoot it with a 12-gauge shotgun. Then he would take three packets of baker's yeast out and sprinkle it on the dead person's head. Next he would urinate on the cadaver's head. This he contended put the bacterial action of the yeast into overdrive and it dissolved everything but the bones in two days' time. Riley described several places he dumped some bodies. Clyde Gleason located a total of six bodies. Two of them he was able to identify. Most all had their faces pulverized by an application of birdshot. One, skeletal identification was made from the serial number found on a stainless steel artificial replacement hip joint. The second was from a name found inside a piece of a lower denture.

Jenkins never kept up with the names of the people he dispatched for Bob Noir. Riley laughed as he told his buddy Clyde Gleason of his yeast and urine disposal system. He said "That was how I did it. Just piss on 'em, I'd tell myself."

An interesting aside in this case was that the machinist-turned-contract-killer was a stand-up guy to the bitter end. He did not relate the story of his misdeeds to the deputy until six weeks after Bob Noir was dead. Similarly he would not give up the name of his cousin the undertaker. There is an expression that blood is thicker than water. This may well be the case—unless you just happen to be a hemophiliac.

TWENTY-SEVEN

....

JUSTICE SERVED WELL DONE

Dante Williams, Jeffery Prejean (aka Hammerhead) and Jamail (Pooky) Wilson were northeast Houston street trash. They were the illegitimate spawn of welfare queens and their life goals were much the same as the sperm donors that helped to produce them. Good sex, good times and no sort of responsibilities could very well have been their mantra. They were adults under Texas law and within eighteen months of one another in age when they were collectively arrested and charged with aggravated (armed) robbery. Though none of these gentlemen could spell the word cat without the letter K, they were all rather street wise. They figured that the high-rent districts should produce victims with thicker wallets and Rolex watches. Their logic had some merit. Willie Sutton (a once highly sought after fugitive) was once asked why he robbed banks. He answered truthfully, "Because that's where they keep the money." What our trio of bandits didn't figure on was a potential victim with both a concealed carry handgun permit and the fact that he was not afraid to use his weapon.

Juan Segovia was the third potential victim of the night that our scholars singled out to jack up for his money, watch and leather jacket. Large four-legged predators look to pull down the weak and most vulnerable of the herd animals they come across. The two-legged hyenas and jackals within our society have much the same orientation. Juan was a slim forty-five-year-old man that stood five feet six inches tall. He drove a white convertible Mustang. On the night in question he was walking with a limp and using a cane because he had injured his knee racing competitively in a Motocross competition. What the street animals took for a well-dressed and smallish grey haired man with a cane turned out to be a Cuban-American version of Doc Holliday with a case of the red ass. What happened next might best be summed up in the recorded statement of the wounded robbery suspect Pooky Wilson that was taken while he was awaiting treatment at Ben Taub Hospital's emergency room.

Partial Transcript—Suspect Jamail Wilson

Ben Taub Hospital   **June 21, 20XX**

"We was out cruisin', me, Hamma-Head and Dante. I don't know where the car that we was in came from at all. I guess somebody musta loaned it to us. We needed to score us some money so we went out to jack us some fat cats out offa Westheimer. We was all gonna do one each and then split the money up even—you know three ways between us. Hamma-Head and Dante had already jacked they folks and it was my turn. I saw this skinny grey headed guy dressed in a white leather coat. He was walkin' with a cane and going through a parking lot. I got out of the car on him and pointed my gun at him. I tol' him to give me his money, watch and car keys. That was when things got real crazy.

He just grins real big at me and says "Oh Yeah?" Then he reached behind him as quick as a cat. I figured he gots something as big or bigger than mines—so I runs like Hell for the car. As I'm getting into the back seat I hear a loud **bam** and I got hit in the back. I fell into the car and Hamma-Head pulls off. I hear *Bam-Bam-Bam-Bam* and glass starts breaking. Hamma-Head started yelling "I'm hit, I'm hit." Then our car crashes into a parked car in the parking lot. The next thing I know I'm getting jerked out the car by my hind legs. I look up and see the guy that just shot me. He starts kicking me in my face and says "Who's got the biggest balls now muther-f--ka?" Then he axed me, "What's wrong—don't you want to play no more bitch?" I will tell you right now officer I

```
was  never  so  happy  in  my  life  to  see  the
laws  pull  up.  That  old  mutha-f--ka  is  cra-
zy."
```

Hammer Head Prejean had the common decency to die at the scene. The 158-grain jacketed hollow-point .38 Super bullet entered the back of his neck and severed his carotid artery. Jamail (Pookey) Wilson cost the taxpayers of Harris County, Texas many thousands of dollars before he became a ward of the state. Dante Wallace confessed to his sins and served seven years of a ten-year sentence.

IPSC style shooting competitors draw from a holster and engage multiple targets with a high rate of speed and accuracy. A thing of beauty is truly a joy to behold and the Cubans dominate the sport in the Florida competition circles. With the coming of concealed carry laws to many states violent street crime has gone down. Colonel Jeff Cooper is credited with saying "America will be a better place when criminals are more afraid of the decent citizens than the decent citizens are of them."

TWENTY-EIGHT

....

MEAT MALLET

Bobby Matthews had a whole six months on the department, and had just come off his probationary status when he was transferred to Fifteen District (now Ten District) and was assigned to the beat car that included Ben Taub Hospital. Once you are assigned the beat car that includes a county or charity hospital, it guarantees you will get to write double the number of reports compared to the rest of the units in your district. Fifteen-Edward-Thirty check the beating victim, the cutting victim, the shooting victim-is all you will hear. Low seniority in a district can guarantee you such an assignment, because nobody wants that beat.

Young Officer Matthews was assigned to check an assault victim named Sammy Lawrence (later determined to be a registered sex offender) that had come in from an unknown location one Friday afternoon. Notepad in hand, our young officer walked into a side treatment room just off the emergency room crash center to interview the fifty-seven-year-old black male. Bobby found the individual in question to be naked from the waist down and in excruciating pain. His penis was mangled and badly swollen and bleeding. When asked what in the world had happened to him, Sammy would only answer: "I don't want to talk about it." Matthews wasn't having such a great day either, but nowhere near as bad as Lawrence. He told Sammy, "That's fine with me Bubba. You see, I'm real tight with the staff here at the hospital. You see until such time as you tell me what happened today, I will see to it that they withhold any treatment. Your beat-up little pecker will simply rot off before a doctor will find the time to treat you, BoBo." At first the reluctant little pervert offered up, "Okay, well maybe I was doing something I shouldn't have and got caught." After a few more minutes, a semblance the truth finally came out.

It was finally determined that Sammy J. Lawrence was both an alcoholic and a weenie waver. Sometimes when he'd had a couple of beers he got the urge to play show and tell with little children. On the day in question he had been so intent upon a group of little children that he failed to notice Momma Bear lurking close by. The weenie waver had been walking down the street and saw a group of boys and girls seated at a table having milk and cookies inside a shotgun shack. It was a warm spring day. The windows in the old frame house were up and there were no screens on its windows. Doofus pulled out his most prized possession and laid it upon the window ledge in an attempt to shock the children in question and to gratify himself. What he did not see, however, was the highly protective mother at the sink washing dishes only three feet from that kitchen window. Mommy Dearest saw what stupid was up to before the kids even noticed him. She then grabbed a meat mallet and hit a home run. Sammy's manly appendage was flattened and mangled badly by the metal spiked grid and the term meat mallet took on a whole new meaning. Mister Lawrence did not see the humor in the young officer laughing and telling him that he was just lucky the lady of the house didn't own a meat cleaver. Cops always enjoy it when justice gets metered out upon the criminal element, because all they ever get to see is the victims.

TWENTY-NINE

FRED'S LIQUOR STORE

Fred Tucker ran a liquor store off Wayside Drive for well over twenty years. He opened the shop ten years after he came back to the states from the Korean War. His return from Asia to Texas saw him minus a few body parts though. He left behind a couple of ribs and a good bit of his left lung, but he came back. When Fred was hit by a very large piece of shrapnel he was well on his way to wearing out his third Browning automatic rifle. The transfer into civilian life from Marine Corps Rifle Squad leader went smooth enough. When he set up shop in the booze business he transferred enemy status from the Communist Chinese troops to local armed robbery suspects. Fred however kept his machine gunner's since of humor. Now however he was the one dictating the rules of engagement.

Fred's Hooch House (as it was called) was all of twelve feet by twenty feet inside. He kept cold beer and wine on one side of the shop and storage on the other end. There were a few shelves with different brands of booze on them in the central ten by twelve-foot section of the store. To get into the shop you had to be buzzed in by somebody at the register. Himself could also throw a switch and lock the front door, holding you hostage if he wanted to. Fred kept a lightweight Colt Commander on his side under one of those square-tailed Mexican shirts that the barbers wear. His weapon of choice was actually a sawed-off shotgun. He always had two shotguns in the shop with him at any given time. One of them was a Model 11 Remington which he brought with him from home and left the business with every night. The second was a Stevens double-barreled affair that was strapped under the sales counter. Both scatterguns were twelve gauges. The Remington was loaded with oo buckshot and the twice barrel was stoked with three-inch number two lead goose loads. Actually Fred had several of the Stevens shotguns, and all of them were the same. Their barrels were cut down so that they were nineteen inches long and they had just enough pistol grip to be well within the legal length guidelines.

Fred's sales counter was directly across from and in line with the store's front door. The sales counter was built out of 2x4 lumber and the countertop was solid one inch thick tongue and groove pine with a plastic laminate top glued to it. The front of the sales counter did not have a solid front right underneath the cash register and for two feet on either side of it. There were only posters advertising either liquor or beer stapled to the 2x4 framing in the area right under the register. This is because Fred had one of his Stevens double barrels wired to the underside of the sales counter. He would aim the shotgun's twin barrels at the middle of the thirty-inch wide entry door and at a height of between three and a half and four feet above the floor. He determined where the shot load's points of impact would be by placing penlight flashlights inside the gun's barrels. Both of the gun's triggers were wired to a large pedal that was affixed to the floor directly under the cash register. It resembled a car's accelerator pedal, only larger. The rig was set up so that you had to stomp the pedal really hard in order to get the gun to go off. That way an accidental discharge was highly unlikely. Naturally the safeties on all of the set guns had been disconnected by a local redneck gunsmith.

Fred's social life was his business. He always kept a coffee pot going until around noon. One of his rat terrier dogs often accompanied him to work. He was closed on Sunday and Monday and closed up early whenever he felt like it. The area cops could always use his bathroom or phone. He tried to stay on a friendly basis with the Park Place officers because he would have to call them out from time to time to pick up some of the trash that tried to rob him. Fred never carried his wallet on his person due to the potential for being robbed. He habitually left it in the trunk of his car. The method he generally used to kill armed robbers that came into his shop was always the same. If they made it into the store and got the drop on him, then he would let them go ahead and rob him. As they were leaving he would proceed and insult them and then shoot them to death. His standard procedure was typically to wait until the robber was trying to exit the front door. Then he would yell out either, "Hey, Nigger" or "Hey, Asshole." When the crook turned around Fred would stomp the pedal under the counter. Both barrels would cut loose at the same time and shoot stupid between the belly button and nipple high. With only poster paper on the counter's front the goose loads became a real meat grinder.

Two of the men Fred killed were not inside his business at the time. One was waiting for him as he exited the store and obviously had not done his homework. The Hooch House man always kept carried his semi-auto Remington 12-gauge with a round in the chamber when he walked from his car to the business or out of the door at night. Double-o (oo) buckshot rehabilitates better than most things. The second man waited for Fred in the bushes beside the driveway at his home. A magazine full of Speer 200 grain hollow-points sent that scholar to the great beyond.

When Fred Tucker did some varmint hunting the cops would come out to take pictures, make diagrams and remove his scatter gun from under the counter. He would have to call one of his VFW buddies to come secure his place. There was a door made of 2x6 lumber that would bolt up to the front of the building if the front glass had also been a casualty that night. Fred would have to go downtown and give another sworn statement as to what had transpired. The next day the store would not open until about noon due to clean up and repairs. Another shotgun would be mounted under the counter and aimed where it would do its best work. Sometimes Fred would have to replace the sheet vinyl flooring also. He originally had stick down 12-inch squares of linoleum on the floor when he first opened the business. It became obvious that blood got into the cracks between the tiles and cleanup was a more difficult task. Sheet vinyl flooring just worked so much better. A new liquor or beer poster would cover the counter front and Fred would add a new trophy to his collection.

His trophies consisted of Polaroid pictures of every robber that he'd had the occasion to kill over the twenty plus years he operated the store. They were kept in a scrapbook that he stored under the counter. He would show them off to his friends and regular customers that would come by to visit. People would come by and he would tell them how each shooting went down. Often he would laugh and point out the startled expressions on some of the dead men's faces as they stared at the camera with their glazed-over eyes.

Fred was shot to death by some unknown person one cold January night. Whoever killed him did not rob him. They just walked up and shot him repeatedly at close range with either a .38 special or .357 magnum Smith & Wesson revolver. Nothing was taken but his life. The only motive anyone could think of was retaliation for one of his many earlier shootings. The case was never cleared and his killer was never identified and brought to justice.

THIRTY

....

MY BEST REGARDS

Emergency room workers, doctors, cops and paramedics develop a dark since of humor as a defense mechanism. Here is one of my favorite stories. A twenty-five year-old misguided child of the streets named Leroy Compton came into Ben Taub Hospital's emergency room by fire department ambulance. He had a wooden handled ice pick buried all the way to the handle in the top of his head. The pick was located in a spot almost perfectly centered in regard to front-to-back and side-to-side measurements. To everyone's amazement the gentlemen in question was lucid and speaking as coherently (under the conditions) as any street animal could be expected to. The x-rays of his head indicated that both spheres of the brain appeared to have been perfectly split and no vital injuries seemed to have occurred.

Leroy had no physical motor or verbal impairment that could be determined. The emergency room doctors were of the opinion that there was little to no permanent injury that might actually result from this stabbing. A highly regarded local surgeon named Robert Alexander was called in for his opinion. He reviewed the x-rays and spoke with the patient. He then called for a stout pair of pliers from the maintenance department. The five-inch long metal spike was pulled from the man's skull. The wound suffered by this mother's son was covered by a one-inch butterfly bandage and Mr. Compton was kept overnight for observation.

The next morning as the good Doctor Bob was making his hospital rounds he stopped in to check on his latest patient, Leroy Compton. Leroy was quite talkative and eating breakfast when the doctor entered his room shortly after daylight. Doctor Alexander checked the man's eyes and motor skills and noted he showed no symptoms of any complications. The patient was then cleared and authorized to be released later that morning.

Bob Alexander (with his off-beat since of humor) always asked his welfare patients the same question. He inquired of his stabbing victim patient, "Leroy, I saved your life last night, do you know that?" To this question the patient answered with a hearty, "Yes Sir." Alexander smiled and got to make his favorite inquiry by saying, "Now considering what all I've done for you—what are you going to give me?" Leroy pondered upon this for a few seconds and with a big grin proudly proclaimed,

"Well sir, I'm just gonna have to give you my best regards."

THIRTY-ONE

....

YOU'RE SURROUNDED

Truman Hebert was a drug addict whose wealthy parents lived in a posh neighborhood called Briargrove. He began using marijuana in the sixth grade. All of his life he had stolen from his family home and forged checks on their checking accounts. Since he was sixteen his parents had spent a modest fortune on drug rehabilitation and counseling. His brother and sister contended that Truman just should have been drowned at birth. This son of the rich (or something closely akin to that) had stolen, forged, and traded family cars for drugs while he was growing up. About age twenty he got into credit card fraud and identity theft to maintain his love affair with drugs. By age twenty-three he had multiple misdemeanor arrests and surprisingly only one state jail felony conviction.

At age twenty-three years and two months, Truman hit the big time. He and another junkie friend of his decided to pull a drug rip off/armed robbery of a mid-level cocaine dealer. Truman Herbert had a shotgun and his hair-brained accomplice brought along a Colt AR-15 that he had just procured in a residential burglary. Both bad boy jackers had to pump up their courage with a hit of methamphetamine before they kicked the dealer's front door in. To say both men were as nervous as a cat with a turpentined butt would be an understatement. The drug dealer's double-wide wife would later describe the suspects as having pinpoint-sized pupils that she proclaimed looked like "Two pee holes in the snow." The bone heads came through the door yelling "Police" and surprised the resident drug dealer as he was sitting on the couch. Yon dealer jumped to his feet when the front door was breached and both of the scholars immediately shot him. He was shot once with the shotgun and three times with the .223-caliber rifle. The rifle was loaded with soft nosed bullets and only one of the three projectiles exited the dearly departed's body.

An interesting aside to this point about the .223 or 5.56mm soft nosed bullet comes from a study done by LAPD SWAT. They found that round to have less over-penetration on a human body than a 9mm hollow-point bullet fired from a handgun. This makes it a better choice to fire in an urban environment than any of the standard handgun cartridges. It did not matter what brands of .223 ammo the urban shooters chose to use, the results were consistently the same. Any soft point configuration seemed to expand so rapidly that all of the hydrostatic shock from the bullet was contained within the carcass of the intended target. The desired result of rehabilitation was almost instantaneous and the target's innards looked rather like Jell-O. Now back to the story-line.

The suspects were not daunted by the murder. They demanded the dope and money—and got some of both. Being the good human hyenas they were, they also sacked up a few valuables they could readily carry and exited through the front door of the house. Unfortunately for them, they happened to run right past another customer and longtime friend of the now late dope dealer. That friend had also gone to high school with both of the mental midgets in question and at one point had run in the same social circles they did. To make things even better this friend/customer chose to hang around and talk to the police. A willing witness is unusual if not unheard of in dope and drug house murders.

Both the Homicide and the Robbery Divisions were sent out to the scene. This sort of case is classified locally as a home invasion. The Robbery Division usually works them when nobody gets killed. There are enough home invasion robberies in Houston that the Robbery Division has designated a specific squad to handle them. Cops also get excited when robbery suspects (called Highjackers in Houston) go around identifying themselves as police and wearing police raid jackets while they commit armed robberies. The Homicide guys worked on the physical scene portion of the case while the Robbery Detectives got the sworn statements and canvassed the area for additional witnesses. The Robbery cops sent the dead man's wart hog wife downtown along with the eye witness that had gone to school with the junkie jackers. With known and named suspects from the scene, there were color photograph lineups (called photo arrays) waiting on the witnesses as soon as they got into the Central Police Station. Positive identifications were made on both suspects and arrest warrants were filed and validated by the 24-hour hearing judge at the county courthouse annex. Truman Hebert and his good friend and co-killer Randy Oliver were both charged with capital murder.

Randy Oliver was found by a patrol unit as he was seated in a stolen car in front of his parent's middle-class home. Randy claimed to know nothing about any robbery or shooting. When he was transported to the Homicide Division one of the detectives asked him where his good friend Truman Hebert was. Oliver said he did not know, but thought Truman might be visiting friends up in the Austin area. On the off-side chance Randy Oliver might be telling a semblance of the truth one of the Homicide investigators called Austin's Homicide unit. There was only one investigator on deck that night. He was named Ray Martinez and he was asked if he could run the wanted suspect Hebert through the city and county systems. The Houston investigator wanted to see if there was any information about the wanted suspect or any known associates of his in the city of Austin or Travis County. The detective gladly ran the misguided Hebert child's name though their system and found a two-year-old traffic warrant under the suspect's name and date of birth. The car he had been driving when the citation was issued was registered to a Dr. Bobby Boyd who lived in a high-rent district not far from Lake Travis.

The address was criss-crossed through a directory and the phone number for that address was determined. That number was answered by a rather effeminate sounding older male who identified himself as Dr. Boyd. Ray Martinez identified himself and he asked Dr. Boyd if he knew a Truman Hebert. The good Doctor answered "Yes that's my grandson, and I happen to be looking right at him right now."

Thinking quickly on his feet, Martinez responded, "Doctor your grandson is wanted out of Houston on a murder charge. What's more, there is a SWAT team surrounding your house at this very moment. I am with the hostage negotiation team and the only way I can guarantee your grandson's safety is if you cooperate with me fully. I will ask you to keep him inside and turn your front porch light on. I will be there in ten minutes and take him into custody. No one needs to get hurt. Please just do as I say and I and promise that no assault will be made upon your house. No doors need to be kicked in and no tear gas canisters need to be fired." The startled alcoholic physician did as he was directed. Ten minutes later Martinez took the bewildered suspect into custody without incident. A good line of BS is a definite asset at times.

THIRTY-TWO

....

PLAY DADDY

In the black community there exists a practice that often confounds white and Hispanic street officers and
investigators alike. This is the practice of claiming
someone as a blood relative even when they are not. It is
a problem that must be worked through to get to real
answers. This quasi-kinship in its applied vernacular
might be called a play family.

An example would be when you are working an assault or shooting case and someone rushes up claiming
to be a family member. Their identification shows a different last name than that of the victim. With the high
rates of illegitimate births in America this is unfortunately not uncommon at all. You as the scene investigator do not want to release information to unknown
persons. That person may have ties to your suspect—
who in turn may simply be trying to determine which
hospital the victim is headed for. Thereby they may be
able to locate your shooting or stabbing victim and fin-

ish the job that he or she started. Further cops try to hoard and hold back information gleaned in the course of their investigations. Sometimes information will come back to you from street sources that only your suspect could have known.

Meanwhile back at the ranch—and back to the problem at hand. Your witnesses and suspects claim kinship and when pressed will sometimes (oftentimes) admit that the party in question is actually their play mother, or play sister, play cousin or play grandmother. It was this phenomenon that two detectives named Harmon and Forrest were trying to explain to a strapping young officer named Tad Williams. Tad had just joined the Crime Scene Unit. He'd been through the basic forty-hour crime scene school and was now riding with an experienced crime scene officer for some on-the-job training.

It was the afternoon of Friday July the 9th when Harmon and Forrest caught a six p.m. murder scene in the 1800 block of Gillette. The location was in the bottoms of the old Fourth Ward in a section known as Freedman's Town. This was an area inhabited (sometime infested) by the descendants of freed slaves and is now just west of downtown and south of Buffalo Bayou. An argument between two professional alcoholics that were neighbors led up to one of them striking the other in the head with a three-foot length of cast iron pipe. The injured sixty-two-year-old victim reportedly dropped like he had been struck from behind with a double-bitted pole axe. Patrol units made the scene and were able to snag the suspect and two relatively sober witnesses. The paramedics transporting the beating victim advised the blue suits (uniformed officers) that the injured man looked closer to terminal than critical. The soon to be dead man was known to the suspect and both witnesses only as Blue Coat, though they had all lived within a block of one another for between fifteen to twenty years. Blue Coat was hauled to Ben Taub Emergency where he was dead upon arrival.

The brand new crime scene officer Tad Williams made the scene with his senior partner Gerald Burque along with the investigators Harmon and Forrest. It was ninety-two degrees in the shade and the humidity rates were even higher. The neighborhood streets were narrow and the local residents hostile. When air temperature and blood temperature come close to one another— it doesn't take much to set people off who are living without air conditioning.

The murder scene was limited to the front yard of the shanty house located in front of XXXX Gillette. The detective and crime scene units both arrived at the same time. There was a single officer holding down the scene, as the other units that made the scene had already hauled the two admitted witnesses and suspect to the

Homicide Division for statements. Even though the cops were not involved in the attack on Blue Coat there was open hostility toward the only present authority figures—the cops.

As the Homicide investigators began trying to put together the scene description and canvas for additional witnesses the senior of the crime scene officers got a call over the radio. He was advised that the fatal beating victim had been identified as having a name other than Blue Coat. The dead man's true name was determined to be Calvin Eugene Williams and he was born December 7th of 1943. When the crime scene officer in training Tad Williams heard this he threw his arms up over his head and bellowed out "Oh Laud—they done kilt my play daddy Calvin."

Under some circumstances Tad's carrying on might have been something laughable. Unfortunately it hit a raw nerve with the crowd that had gathered. Harmon later would say that the scene reminded him of the shield-beating episode of the native warriors in the movie Zulu. Forrest told the crime scene officers to estimate the distances, take two Polaroid pictures so he could describe the scene and to pick up the pipe that one wino clobbered the other with. Then they cleared out. The crime scene officers were told to come back the following day at the first part of their shift to get their measurements for the scene diagram. It was a practice case anyway. Harmon was thoroughly pissed off. They'd caught the scene fairly early in their shift and there wasn't really anyway to drag the investigation out to justify even one hour of paid overtime. He claimed that was the biggest crime committed that day. Albert held to the concept that anything worth doing right was worth doing for overtime money. Forrest claimed that Harmon could be on a scene for fifteen minutes and accurately tell you how much paid overtime he thought he could milk from that investigation. He also claimed that Harmon's mother had been scared by a cash register shortly before she gave birth to him. Bob Forrest thought that had to be the reason Harmon was such a money grubbing tightwad old bastard.

The murder suspect Cleveland Epps gave a confession wherein he admitted to hitting Tad Williams' play daddy in the head with a piece of scrap iron. It appears Blue Coat had spoken poorly of Cleveland's mother. The high point of Epps' confession was when he stated "Blue Coat never up and died before just because somebody came upside his head with something."

THIRTY-THREE

....

POLISH EXCHANGE POLICEMEN

Albert Harmon and Sherwood Yost rode the late night shift out of the Central Station in 17 District. They were both hulking brutes of men and neither had to worry about being approached to appear on recruiting posters or about becoming male models. When they rode together there was in excess of five hundred pounds of cop in their car. They both however loved their jobs and looked forward to any chance at getting into devilment. Seeking amusement caused them to look for trouble. As such their crime statistics were some of the highest in the district. When things got slow they would always looked for ways to entertain themselves.

One night Harmon came up with the idea of becoming Pivo Walensa, the Polish exchange policeman. He and Sherwood put together the ten to fifteen words they collectively knew of Polish, Czech, and Russian to put their latest plan into action. In as much as their beat was called Queer Town in the lower Westheimer area they hardly ever ran out of oddwads and wackos to mess with.

Harmon would take the name plate off of his uniform shirt and take on the identity of Pivo Walensa. His standard approach was to stop a car and approach it saying in a thick eastern European accent, "Saframinski, need to see lisencia please. I have stop-ped you for having a bad tail light." He would converse with the violator and Sherwood would stand by to translate if need be. Violators were either very helpful and spoke slowly and clearly or they would react with comments like "You guys will just about hire anybody these days won't you."

Not to be outdone, Sherwood became Officer Gay Blade, the Montrose District policeman. Officer Gay Blade would swish and mince around when writing tickets or while gathering information for offense reports. Harmon told Sherwood he did the swish routine entirely too well and sometimes it made him question if Yost might in fact be a switch hitter or a closet case. Sherwood answered that his 28-inch hickory nightstick was really a phallic symbol and if Albert was good he could stroke it for him. All of this role-playing by the two class clowns was good for entertainment up until Ruby Samuels got beaten up by her now late common-law husband.

Ruby made for call for service about midnight after she got punched in the face by her half drunken live-in boyfriend named Anson Green. Anson was smart enough to leave the house now that he had really pissed her off. Officer Walsensa interviewed the domestic assault victim and made a report, giving her a case number and advising her that if she wanted to file charges she could go to the municipal courts at 1400 Lubbock Street in the morning. Miss Ruby inquired of the kindly exchange policeman what he would do if someone like her estranged husband had blackened his eye. Pivo Walensa answered in his best broken English, "I vood not take dat stuff offa him. I vood get me da biggest butcher knife in da house and I vood stick him in da tripe—dat is vot I vood do." Unfortunately for all of the parties concerned that is just exactly what Ruby did later that night. Anson had cooled off after drinking a beer and walking for about an hour. Ruby kept looking in the mirror at her black eye and she just got madder and madder.

When the cutting/ambulance call dropped at Ruby and Anson's humble abode, Harmon and Yost had enough sense not to check by. Ruby told the Homicide detectives why she had stabbed her stud duck: "Why I only done like that nice foreign talkin' officer said to when he came by earlier in the evening." Ruby had no criminal history and Anson Green was an old time crook with multiple arrests for domestic violence. With a bit of coaching Ruby feared for her safety and was sure she was going to receive a more serious beating the second time around. That is why she used the knife—strictly as a means of self-defense.

The homicide case was referred to a grand jury without charges. Anson was shipped off to the morgue for processing like the swine he actually was. It was just a practice case anyway, because nobody really cared. In Harris County, Texas it is justifiable homicide whenever a wife beater gets shot, stabbed, folded, spindled or mutilated in the course of marital problems. The Polish exchange policeman Pivo Walensa and Officer Gay Blade, however, left town the night Anson Green died at the hands of his beloved shack job. They were never to return to the streets of Houston.

The final ruling in this case by a grand jury in Houston six weeks later was *justifiable homicide*. Unofficially it was classified a NHI case—No Human Involvement determined.

THIRTY-FOUR

....

POOR OLD WILLIE

July 2, 19XX, Central Dispatch, 1830 Hours: Any unit clear and close to make the shooting/ambulance call in Sixteen Adam Twenty's beat. XX02 Calumet—Advise on backup.

The two-man unit with M.D. (Mad Dog) Bell and Andy Riesner aboard jumped the call and arrived in time to momentarily speak with a wounded skinny forty-year-old male named Willie Washington. When the blue suits pulled up the victim was seated on the front steps of a shotgun shack being treated by the two man crew of Medic 20. The injured man was quickly loaded into the waiting fire department ambulance. Willie had an obvious entry and no exit type gunshot wound to his left shoulder. It was also very obvious that the man was in a whole lot of pain. His discomfort still didn't keep him from being evasive when the officers asked him who it was that shot him and where he was when it happened. Any question asked other than name, rank and serial number got an "I don't know" answer. It was obvious to the cops he was lying—but his reason for doing so was puzzling.

While Willie was being strapped onto a gurney by the paramedics a 275-pound woman named Chastity Wood (clad in shorts and a tube top) waddled up. She began caterwauling and wailing. "Willie! What's happened to my poor old Willie?" She was advised he had been shot in the shoulder and that his vital signs were good and it appeared that he was going to pull through the whole ordeal just fine. Willie was loaded into the back of the ambulance and his beloved Chastity (though uninvited) bounded into the back of the ambulance with amazing agility.

With the victim being loaded and being transported the cops followed the blood trail from the front porch back into the house. There they found a .38 snub nosed revolver on the floor in close proximity to where the blood trail began. A search of the house came up with no living beings other than roaches so the blue suits snatched up the gun and followed the ambulance to Ben Taub hospital. They wanted to see if Willie would impart more information about what had really taken place.

Willie was stable so both of the paramedics decided to pile into the front of the ambulance. Besides, Chastity took up most of the back end of their unit and her body odor funk was strong enough to cause a buzzard to puke in a high wind. The air conditioning unit was not working on the paramedic's assigned wonderful piece of city equipment either. Therefore the firemen rolled down their windows and cranked up their sirens as they headed for nearby Ben Taub (The Tub) Hospital. When they arrived at the emergency room Chastity bounded out of the back of the meat wagon encouraging the paramedics to please hurry up because "Poor Old Willie ain't lookin' too good."

The two uniformed officers pulled into the parking lot just as Willie was being rolled through the back doors of the hospital. They passed Chastity who was quietly standing just outside the county hospital's back doors. The cops walked into the crash room of the emergency treatment center just as Willie was being pronounced dead upon arrival. The Doctor pronouncing him dead exclaimed, "Man, look at all those stab wounds! I am just amazed this man was actually still alive long enough for you guys to load him into the ambulance."

The two cops looked at Willie's chest and noted a bunch of bloody dots all over his chest. Without saying a word they both sprinted for the emergency room doors. They jumped into their patrol car and began their search for Chastity Wood. They found her two blocks east of the hospital and walking as fast as her short little tree trunk legs would carry her. Poor Willie's beloved still had her trusty ice pick in her purse when they arrested her. It would later test positive for her old man's blood.

Bell normally never showed any signs of having the milk of human kindness in his soul regarding the plight of his fellow man. This case, however, made him shudder as he thought about Willie and how he died. There he was—strapped down and immobilized as his wart hog common law wife stabbed him over twenty times. He wondered if the suspect covered her victim's mouth with her off hand as she stabbed him over and over again. It was either that or his screams and moans simply went unheard—drowned out by the wailing of the twin sirens on the city ambulance. **Poor Old Willie.**

....

THIRTY-FIVE

PROBABLE CAUSE STATEMENTS

To arrest and charge someone with a crime, probable cause is required. When you go to file a warrant to arrest someone that is not in custody you need to state in the application to the court what facts you have that cause you to believe a certain person committed a specific criminal act inside the confines of that court's jurisdiction. Similarly when you have observed a crime committed in your presence then your charge paperwork must detail the probable cause that existed to support your arresting the suspect and the charge you are filing. Here are two probable cause statements that are both entertaining and interesting. The first statement is an in-custody situation. The second is a warrant application called a to-be warrant.

Mark Twain is credited with saying, "The human animal is the only one that blushes, or needs to." These two actual statements are good examples that Mr. Twain knew what he was talking about. What's more, nobody could ever make these sorts of things up.

SUMMARY OF FACTS (AN IN-CUSTODY SITUATION)

At approximately 0325 hours, a driver now identified as the defendant, John Doe, was operating a red 2001 Oldsmobile four-door sedan (Texas plate XXXXXX) in the 4000 block of the South Sam Houston Parkway, eastbound in lane number one. The defendant failed to maintain a single lane and crossed the inside warning line and struck the concrete dividing barricade. The vehicle then rolled over onto its roof and skidded eastbound approximately 310 feet before coming to a stop in the 4200 block of South Sam Houston Parkway (toll lane).

I observed the vehicle was upside-down, and the defendant was upside-down and inside the vehicle. The defendant was seat-belted securely into the driver's seat. The driver was alert and removed his seatbelt and was able to exit the vehicle through the driver's side window.

The defendant appeared to be confused about the accident. I observed his pants to be unfastened and a plastic/rubber type inflatatable love doll was lying across the center console and the passenger seat with the upper torso towards the rear of the vehicle. I asked the defendant if he was injured and he replied, "No". He realized that his pants were unfastened and hanging loose around his waist and he asked "Can we keep this a secret between us?"

I smelled a strong odor of alcoholic beverage emitting from his breath as he spoke and I noticed his balance was very poor. I had the defendant sit in the rear of my patrol car while waiting for Houston EMS to arrive. The defendant advised that he had placed his vehicle on cruise control and was engaged in a sexual act with the love doll when he lost control of the vehicle and struck the concrete barrier. The HFD Medic 46 arrived on the scene and checked the defendant. The defendant signed a refusal to be transported to a hospital to be checked, stating "I'm fine—not hurt."

The defendant was placed in custody for DWI. I transported the defendant to the Clear Lake substation and read him the DIC 24 form which he agreed to provide a specimen of breath to be tested. Analysis of the specimen displayed the defendant's blood-alcohol level concentration was .236 and .229 at 0455 hours (one and one-half hours after the accident). I videotaped the defendant performing the SFST and on each test he performed he did very poorly. The tape would be placed into evidence and submitted to the district attorney's office. Assistant District Attorney Miller accepted charges for DWI. The vehicle was towed by Egret Wrecker #35 and placed into storage at XXXX Old Galveston Road.

PROBABLE CAUSE STATEMENT: HARASSING COMMUNICATIONS

Your affiant, J. P. Virgil, is a City of Houston police officer assigned to the Family Violence Unit of that agency. He was assigned to investigate Houston police incident report number 13752306 and has reason to believe that Richard Paul Doran, hereafter named the defendant, did on or about January 17 of 20XX commit the offense of *harassing communication* in Harris County, Texas.

Your affiant spoke with the complainant in this case, Johnnie Faith Smithers. She stated that a person known to her for a period of three weeks and named Richard Paul Doran had been harassing her by telephone of a period on one full week. The defendant called the complainant's home on January 17, 20XX and the complainant tape recorded that conversation at the affiant's request. That conversation is inclusive of the following verbiage:

You know what? You a sorry trifling-ass bitch, you know what I'm saying? You ain't got no motherf**king idea what is in front of you, and if you ready to get mother**king rid of it, you know what I'm saying? F**k you and your sorry trifling, trick, bitch, soft porn, poon-ass, bullshit-ass, mother**king-ass bitch! F***you for life bitch.

The complainant stated that she was very offended by the defendant's vulgar remarks and she feared for her personal safety. The defendant called the complainant Smithers' apartment, even though on the tape the defendant Doran acknowledges the complainant had earlier asked him not to call her again. The offense occurred in XXXX Broadway in apartment number 4732, a location inside both the city of Houston, and inside of Harris County, Texas.

Mark Twain was clearly right on target.

THIRTY-SIX

....

PSYCHOS ARE US

There exists a class of scary individuals in our world that the British so aptly describe when they say that he or she *should have been drowned at birth*. In nature, puppies or kittens with personality flaws are often killed by the mother animal. There are similarly defective humans that have flaws in their mental makeup that make them dangerous to society. The four-legged animals, when saved from their mothers, are generally found just not to be right, and often they turn out to be downright dangerous when they mature. Unfortunately it is not until humans begin to mature that the true inner beast shows itself. The less intelligent of these folks cannot hide their dark side and become institutionalized early on if society gets lucky. The good intelligent psychopath learns early on that he cannot share his feelings with the world. After he bears his soul the first time (and the world gets an inkling as to what lives inside his head and heart) he does not come out of his shell again. He would like a friend that can relate to him, and occasionally these creatures run up on a sicko they can run with for a time.

The following is the statement of a highly dangerous and intelligent young man. He had never been arrested as an adult. He had been sent to some psychological counseling by his family a few years before. He learned not to tell anyone about his true feelings, as he'd learned he would scare people and draw unwanted attention to himself. He was seventeen and in high school when he was arrested for stabbing a young lady he took out on a date.

The investigator that was assigned to this case was exceptional at interrogation. The suspect related well to him. The suspect provided a very damning confession which gave a quick look into the kid's twisted thought processes. He was then shuffled off into the court and jail system. If he survived the prison ordeal he would never again to let anyone know what was going on inside his mind, nor would he ever again confess to a crime.

See the attached confession for what will likely be the only time this subject will open up to tell another person about how he thinks and feels. He was intelligent and made good grades. He very likely will never again make the same costly mistake again—confessing, that is. Make no mistake—if given the chance he *will* stab someone again, because he liked doing it.

Statement of Person in Custody

State of Texas   County of Harris
April 23, XXXX   Time: 5:30 PM

Prior to the making of this statement I, Marvin Lee Powell, have been warned by Sgt. J. H. Benson, the person to whom I am giving this statement that:

1. I have the right to remain silent and not make a statement and that any statement I make may be used against me.
2. I have the right to have an attorney present to represent me prior to and during the making of this statement. If I cannot afford an attorney, one will be appointed for me free of charge.
3. I have the right to terminate this interview at any time.
4. I have read and understand these rights and waive them to make this voluntary statement.

I am in the Homicide Division of the Houston Police Department. I was arrested last night from my parent's house. I was arrested because I stabbed a girl named Patty Sue Crabb. I met her at the Alternative School at Springwoods High School. I am doing two weeks at the A. School because I got caught at a football game with a large pocket knife. I am not sure why Patty Sue is in the A School program.

I have always loved knives and I think a lot about cutting or stabbing people. As a little kid I used to love the Jason movies. Sometimes after dark I would put on my Jason hockey mask and with a knife in each hand I would chase cars down the street in our neighborhood. Day before yesterday I asked Patty Sue out for a pizza and a movie. After the movie we got in my dad's car and she slid over next to me. We kissed and I got this overpowering desire to cut her throat. I had a Hitler Youth reproduction knife under my sweater. After we kissed a couple of times I stuck her in the neck with my knife. She screamed and jumped out of the car. She ran away screaming and toward the theater we'd just left. I got scared and drove off. I tried to stab her in the jugular vein. If I had connected I am sure she would have died very quickly. I must have missed. This is my first attempt at killing someone and I messed it up.

_____

Signature of person making statement

Author's Note:

A short look into the mind of such an individual causes you to wonder just how many like him are out there functioning and coexisting with you in your everyday life. I fear you should forever trust in the Lord but keep your powder dry.

THIRTY-SEVEN

OH LUCY

Russell Houck was a police transplant to Texas from southern Louisiana. He came from a law enforcement family there. His father was a retired state trooper and his brother is still out there on the interstate. Rusty was a deputy sheriff in his home parish for five years when he got recruited by Houston P.D. He crossed the Sabine River in pursuit of a bigger paycheck. As he so aptly put it, "I had a desire to stop living on red beans and rice and start eating steak regularly." Houck always had enjoyed life to the fullest. His wife Raylene claimed that if Rusty had a serious bone in his body it was a barbequed rib bone that he held in his hand and that he was seriously chewing the meat off of it.

The priorities in Russell Houck's life were his wife and kids, followed by cooking, hunting and fishing. Houck's mother was a full-blooded Cajun and she understood hunting, fishing as well as good times and good food. As soon as you met Rusty's mom you knew where he got his outlandish and rather colorful since of humor. Whenever someone would call one of Marie Houck's kids a Coonass, she would set them straight right quick. She would tell them "Don't you be callin' my baby no Coonass. I'll have you know Mister Houck is a white man and he ain't got no Coonass blood in him at all. The Coonass blood comes from my side of the family. That only makes Rusty or Michael or Shana only half-assed."

Russell rode patrol out of the Westside Station, and after four years there he was promoted to sergeant. He worked the 3 p.m. to 11 p.m. shift by choice, as it fit his personality. He was one of the few people that liked daytime television, as it contained the old comedy series he so dearly loved. Lucille Ball and the Beverly Hillbillies were his favorites. Raylene claimed the Clampetts resembled people she met at the yearly Houck family reunions. She would go on to tell people that among that crowd the outdoor cooking of a pig over an open fire and the making up of a five-gallon pot of beans had a sort of a family cult following.

When Houck promoted to the rank of sergeant he was transferred to the Beechnut Station. This is a very common practice to not put a new supervisor over people he just partnered with. The Beechnut troops took to their new sergeant with a wild since of humor. He liked working and supported the officers that were hard chargers and wanted to put crooks in jail. Rusty had a talent at defusing high-tension situations with his good-old-boy way of talking. He could have irate drunks laughing and family feuds simmered down in short order. Ten weeks after his promotion he was called out by some blue suits to make a sergeant-type decision. They'd answered a call about a possible suicidal woman in the Robindale subdivision located near the intersection of Beechnut and Hillcroft streets. A husband and his two small children had just rushed home from a shopping trip after Hubby had been called on his cell phone by his wife. She was threatening to kill herself. He said she's suffered from depression for two years following the birth of their second child. To make matters worse she'd been laid off her job and had to be put on anti-depressant medication. The man of the house also advised that he kept a loaded revolver in the top of his bedroom closet and that his wife knew where it was and also knew how to use it.

Rusty spoke to the husband and determined that the wife's name was Lucille Davis, that she was twenty-eight years old and was told she had taken her medication that morning. In his typical way of trying to defuse the emotionally-charged situations the good Sergeant Houck decided to use humor to try and communicate with the lady in question. He got the front door keys from the husband, and upon opening the front door called out in his best Ricky Ricardo imitation, "Oh Lucy, I think you got some 'splaining to do." His attempt at getting her attention was followed by a single gunshot that ended the life of the lady known as Lucille Davis.

Rusty Houck took the young mother's suicide very hard. He even attended her funeral. After a few days of watching his own depressed state, his wife sent him to the Psychological Services Unit of the Houston Police Department. Russell (to her surprise) went without an argument. It took a while for the old Rusty to resurface, but from then on he never tried to use humor again to defuse a highly tense situation. There had been multiple victims out there on the day Lucille Davis took her life.

THIRTY-EIGHT

....

RAUL

Roy Garza was not the sharpest pencil in the box but somehow he made it through the Houston Police Academy. He did not stay on the street long before everybody determined he was a screw-up. He made it off probation and was assigned to work the night shift out of the Central station. His immediate supervisor, Sergeant Bob Haynie, one night checked by with the new kid on a theft in progress call off 75th and Harrisburg. Bob heard several gunshots while he was still two blocks away from the scene. He pulled up and saw Garcia standing in the street beside his patrol car and reloading his .357 revolver. Sergeant Haynie asked his new rookie, "Roy did you just shoot at someone?" Garcia responded proudly, "Yes Sergeant, they were stealing garbage cans." Bob Haynie was astounded and shouted, "Garza—You don't shoot at people for stealing garbage cans! What in the Hell is the matter with you?" A very indignant Officer Roy Garza blurted out, "But those were *new* garbage cans, Sergeant!"

Roy was transferred to the jail division shortly thereafter, where he remained for eight years until he was promoted to sergeant following a class-action discrimination lawsuit. As a supervisor, Roy did not last long on the street on his second attempt at being a policeman. Then it was back to the jail once more. For many years the city jail was the ceremonial burial ground for the Houston Police Department. New supervisors were rotated through there, but the senior problem child officers and idiot supervisors were buried there.

After his return home to the jail division Roy took on the role of social activist. For several hours of his shift Sergeant Garza would stand at the back door of the jail. He thought there was too much brutality directed toward incoming prisoners on the evening shift. If it looked to him like a prisoner was about to be struck he would storm up to the officers bringing him in and shout, "Don't you dare hit that prisoner. If you do I'll file on you myself in federal court for violating his civil rights!" All of this while he was wagging his finger in some uniformed officer's face.

Some officers on the Tactical Squad broke the good sergeant of his social activist ways. They checked around and determined that he was usually standing his post inside the jail entry doors between eight and nine every night. They would go out and actively seek out some bad-ass drunk to arrest. Then they would do all they could to the prisoner to fire him up before bringing him into the jail. Upon determining Roy was standing by the entry door, they would taunt the drunk and get him fighting mad. The suspect would be removed from the patrol car and have his handcuffs removed. Then one of the officers would walk the uncuffed prisoner to the jail with one arm pinned up behind his back and the officer's other arm around his throat. As soon as the fighting mad drunk was hustled through the back door the officer in question would shove him into the awaiting civic-minded Roy Garza. It only took three times of getting knocked on his ass for Roy to learn he needed to stay away from the jail entry door. After that Garza opted to resign himself to administrative duties and forget social activism.

When it became politically astute to get ethnic and become a Mexican, Roy changed his name to Raul Garza. He then went and bought two wigs and had his teeth capped with bright white porcelain. He retired from Houston P.D. and entered the world of politics. He retired after twenty years as a county constable. He retired the second time somewhat wealthier, but he was truly none the wiser by all accounts.

THIRTY-NINE

....

ROCKY AND THE NFL

When Hurricane Katrina hit New Orleans, Louisiana in 2005 the city of Houston became host to two hundred thousand refugees. Twenty thousand of those unfortunate individuals were unfortunately (for us) confirmed career criminals. When the busloads of refugees fleeing the storm pulled up to the Astrodome, Houston's cops greeted the new arrivals with pump shotguns. The cops would rack a round into the shotgun's chamber as they stepped onto the bus and yelled out "All the dope, all the guns, on the floor NOW!" The center aisles of the buses were littered with both guns and drugs. All the mothers and children were instructed to remain seated. All of the buses' male occupants were instructed to put their hands on their heads and they were extracted from the vehicles one at a time and searched. The evacuees were housed in the Astrodome and a convention center near downtown for several weeks before they were dispersed throughout the Houston area.

Many of the evacuees were products of the government welfare housing projects which the city of New Orleans worked so diligently to hide from the tourist trade. Not only have the projects been infamous for their violence and drug dealing, but also for their inhabitant's hostile attitude toward any and all authority figures. The levels of violence found in the New Orleans projects has been hard for normal humans to fathom unless you view it from the context of life in the sewer. In Orleans Parish, Louisiana the local politicians do not concern themselves much with black people other than at election time. Black-on-black crime is not something to be concerned with generally. Prior to the massive hurricane named Katrina, a full seventy percent of the murder charges filed in Orleans Parish were dismissed prior to those cases ever going to trial.

The local New Orleans residents, in fact, knew all too well that if you talked to the police, the killer you fingered had a seven in ten chance of meeting you on the street in as little as four to six months. Welfare and crime were bred into the population in question to the extent that many people stayed in the city as the storm approached because they were waiting on their welfare checks to arrive. One must have priorities in one's life you know. When the displaced Louisiana children were put in Houston's public school system they could not compete even in the lowest income areas. The kids coming out of the Crescent City were street wise as hell, but they were special education when it came to a scholastic comparison. Keep in mind that Houston does not have the greatest reputation statewide as an educational powerhouse. There were multiple fights and disturbances with the refugee kids claiming they were being called stupid or dumb by their classmates. The local students began calling the Louisiana imports *Nolas*—short for New Orleans. In short order the title was further shortened to *NFLs*. The acronym stood for *Niggas From Louisiana*. Houston's cops picked up on the phrase in very short order and it stuck.

The crime rates soared and the district attorney's office and the Harris county court system became swamped with the refuse from Nawlins. The numbers of armed robberies, rapes and murders went through the roof. The street trash thought they had found the Promised Land. They could not, however, grasp that Houston was not going to put up with their ways or attitudes. The crooks understood that they would get arrested. What they couldn't understand was that they were staying in jail and then going to prison. The snotty attitude of the lower class New Orleans street trash toward authority figures (be they cops or courts) did not fare well for them on Texas' Gulf Coast. Transplants to Houston as young as ten years of age were mouthy and would readily fight with uniformed police when confronted or even when they were simply stopped for questioning.

Edward Holcombe was an officer assigned to Houston's North Command Station. He was a would-be Rambo and always carried at least three guns on or about his person. There was also always a combat knife strapped to one of his spit-shined combat boots. Ed was called Rocky by his night shift coworkers. He as not so called because he bore any likeness to the Sylvester Stallone's boxing movie character. Instead he was given the nickname after his likeness to the flying squirrel in the Rocky and Bullwinkle cartoon series. He was also the only person on the department known to have a bayonet lug installed on his 870 Remington riot gun.

Chucky and Atari Taylor were first cousins and confirmed criminal welfare system Nola's. Their social security numbers were obtained to get benefits not for tax paying purposes. These two gentlemen were too stupid to be con men. Theft and armed robbery was the path they chose. They first came to the attention of the Houston Police Department during an armed robbery of a convenience store. The store they chose to rob was on Crosstimbers Street and twelve blocks east of Interstate 45. Officer Rocky Holcombe (riding a one-man unit) was driving west on Crosstimbers when he spotted the Taylor cousins sacking up cartons of cigarettes from behind the store's checkout counter. Rocky turned his squad car around to see the gentlemen in question exiting the store with garbage sacks of goodies over their shoulders carried in a Santa Claus-like fashion. The two scholars then jumped into a waiting ragged out Oldsmobile and sped off with Officer Holcombe in hot pursuit. Chucky was not NASCAR material and tried a U-turn, hit a curb and blew out a front tire just a half block from the North Freeway (I-45). The Nola cousins abandoned ship and ran north behind a rather large strip shopping center.

Rocky put out the short chase, followed by advising the dispatcher of the suspects' wreck and then their direction of travel on foot. He pulled into the parking lot as the crooks ran through it. He then closed the distance with his car as they sprinted away. The suspects ran north and west and then ran into an alcove in the building behind a restaurant named Aunt Bea's. Chucky Taylor (unknown to Holcombe at the time) was the only one of the crooks that was armed. He jumped into a 55-gallon barrel that was just inside the alcove in question. Rocky pulled up in his patrol car and bailed out of it with his riot gun. He had lost sight of Chucky so he confronted Atari at a distance of about forty feet. Holcombe ordered the juvenile highjacker to the ground. Atari Taylor would not obey, but held his hands up and palms out as he started sidestepping to his right. This made no sense to the cop as the crook was going into a blind alley.

What Atari was in fact doing was moving so that Ed Holcombe would have to follow him. In doing so he put Ed in a position that Chucky could get a clear shot at him.

Rocky slowly followed along after the sidestepping suspect, the whole time covering Atari with his shotgun. Rocky carried the scattergun up against his hip John Wayne style rather than putting the gun butt to his shoulder. When Ed finally moved into a position the adult crook liked, then Chucky opened fire upon the unsuspecting officer. Chucky's hiding place had been picked out hurriedly and was in fact a 55-gallon metal drum that was at least one half full of used cooking grease. As soon as Holcombe started drawing fire he spun around and began firing back. He was shooting from the hip at a suspect that was in the neighborhood of twenty-five feet away. Ed's first load of buckshot went wide and to the right. The nine 31-caliber pellets went into a metal storage building and killed an ice machine inside it. His second load of buckshot went to the left of the well-lubed suspect and hit the other end of the same storage building, this time killing a one hundred pound sack of Idaho potatoes. The third shotgun blast went high and oo buckshot whistled through both sides of the roof of the now mortally wounded sheet metal building and into a brick wall behind it.

Holcombe finally put the shotgun butt to his shoulder and center punched the barrel that Chucky Taylor was squatted down inside of. Chucky had successfully gotten off four rounds at the luckiest police officer in Harris County Texas that night. The whole pattern of pellets hit at the base of Stupid's breast bone and he absorbed a huge number of foot-pounds of energy. The metal drum fell over, spilling the newly-sainted Chucky Taylor and grease onto the driveway. The world was now a better place because another Philistine had been smote hip and thigh and had now been rehabilitated permanently. The taxpayers of America should have shouted Hallelujah for the savings they were to receiving by way of a 12-gauge Remington shotgun that very night.

When the pair of investigators from Homicide (Harmon and Forrest) pulled up at the shooting scene they knew they had a winner in the way of a shooter. Rocky was grinning and giving high-fives to every officer he saw, and wanting to give any and everybody a blow-by-blow description of how it all went down. The shooting was a cut-and-dried situation. The clerk that had been robbed made a positive identification of the dead man as the one who put the gun to his head and the juvenile as the one who kicked him in the groin and shoved him into the beer cooler.

Forrest and Harmon were a couple of men who had maybe one half of an ounce compassion between them.

They stood looking at the shooting scene for any possible additional evidence when Harmon pointed to the newly sainted NFL and inquired, "Do you know what that piece of dung on the ground really represents?" Forrest ventured a guess in the form of, "Urban renewal, or maybe birth control?" Harmon came back with, "Maybe urban renewal, but birth control is out of the question. If you are gonna cull the numbers in a population you're gonna have to kill off some does. One buck can breed a whole lot of does. Now Partner, the way I got this figured it can go one of two ways. Either that officer dropping the stupid bastard in the grease, or maybe he has just killed a janitor in a drum. Being the senior investigator I'm gonna let you make the call on this one."

FORTY

···

SPELL CHECK IS NOT ALWAYS
YOUR FRIEND

To be hired onto the Houston Police Department you are required to meet some minimum standards. You must have either two years of college or a high school education and prior military service. The entrance testing, however, requires only a sixth-grade reading comprehension ability. Prior to coming up with this standard you needed either a high school education or a GED. It was then required that you could at least read at the minimum of a tenth grade comprehension level. Cadets at one time were sifted out of the police academy, sometimes to the level of ten or twenty percent. Now hardly anyone is ever terminated from the ranks of the cadets.

One cadet in the last five years was detained (arrested) on three occasions for family violence while he was still in the academy. Somehow things seemed to get glossed over and he was always returned to the classroom. It took less than a year after his graduation to get him indicted for such an offense and to lose his peace officer's commission with the state after his conviction. The black eye the department got in the media and from the man-hating feminist groups did us very little good either. Another cadet with a master's degree from a Louisiana University known for its football program was actually terminated. It was not because he could not write a complete sentence, neither was it for his very well-documented love of street prostitutes.

Finally when Home Fries was busted out for the last time (while still in the academy) he was consorting with pavement princesses and found to be carrying a pistol. Four times before when he had been rousted by the street cops the police academy had done nothing— although they were notified each time. The fifth time, he was carrying a pistol and the street cops had a reason to arrest him. He told the uniformed troops he was working undercover while still assigned to the academy. The academy could not run interference for him with the district attorney's office, thankfully.

The police department went to laptop computers several years back. Officers now download their reports into the department's computer mainframe at the end of their shift. To clear up the wealth of typographical errors, spell check was added to the laptop units. The major problem that still exists is that cops still need to know how to both spell and read in order to know which options to pick. Possibly the best example of this is the excerpt taken from a scene summary of an offense report. The report was entitled Assault-Bodily Injury-Family Violence. The report's page eight screen listed a summary of events and the officers' names, their payroll numbers and unit number. This is a true rendition of one such screen of a Houston Police offense report.

COMPLS (complainants) STATED THAT THEY WERE INVOLVED IN A VERBAL ARGUMENT THAT EJACULATED INTO A PHYSICAL ASSAULT BY CONTACT SITUATION. NEITHER PARTY WANTED TO FILE CHARGES AT THIS TIME.

NO SUSPECTS/ NO WITNESS/ NO INJURIES

Author's Note: We have met the enemy, and he is us.

FORTY-ONE

······································

STAKE-OUT SQUADS

Stake out squads are sometimes called shotgun squads. They exist to wait for armed robbery suspects. The officers' role is to either arrest or to kill the suspects. Stake out duty is without a doubt at times the most boring detail that could be drawn. You either sit inside a surveillance van or hidden off in a car with tinted windows waiting for a crook to show up. Sometimes you sweat your guts out, and other times you freeze your assets off. You generally work in seedy parts of town. You get flea-bitten and have roaches and rats run across your shoes. There is only one major attraction drawing officers to go to a stake out squad. When you join such a unit, the odds of your either killing or being forced to kill someone will increase dramatically.

The officers who work these squads have certain attributes. They have a sniper's mentality and are talented when it comes to the use of firearms, and they must also have tremendous patience. You have to sit and wait for hours at a robbery hot spot location. You may be behind a one way mirror or parked outside some store, just waiting. It is a tedious and drawn-out job. You just hope that your partner did not dine in beans for lunch. Glamorous it ain't. Los Angeles, New York City and Atlanta all have had stake out squads at one time or another. They may have called them something else, but they were simply stake out squads. Some security companies in Houston set up shotgun squads using off-duty police officers from cities in close proximity to Houston. They typically work for a chain of convenience stores or dry cleaners that have been plagued by multiple armed robbery incidents. Houston officers are, however, forbidden from working robbery stakeout as off-duty security extra jobs.

There exists an American urban legend about a stake out squad shooting that bears repeating. Multiple cities have been credited with being the location of this alleged incident. The event has been alleged to have taken place on either March 31st or on April 1st. The suspect was supposedly being sought following a long series of armed robberies of area liquor stores. The officers involved were supposed to be either behind a curtain or a display of some sort. There was only the shop keeper and a derelict wino-type individual who were in the store when the robbery suspect burst through the front door. He was brandishing a handgun and demanding money when he was summarily dispatched by the officer who was carrying a shotgun.

Homicide comes out and conducts their investigation. The officers and shop owner gave statements regarding the armed suspect entering the store and acting wild and dangerous. They all related that the officer with the 12-gauge identified himself and shot the suspect only when the suspect turned toward that officer with the gun still in his hand. The street person is credited with giving a more colorful rendition of the events. It goes like this:

I was on the liquor store checking out the prices on some wine. This idiot white dude comes through the door calling everybody all kinda mother***ers and waving a pistol around. Out of nowhere a big guy with a bulletproof vest and a shotgun showed up. I'm still not sure where the hell he came from. I hear him yell out "April Fool's Motherf***er" just before he blasted the man one time with that shotgun.

Did it really happen? Who knows.

FORTY-TWO

··

BLOOD LINES RUN TRUE

Sometimes good people can come from a genetic cesspool, but not very often. Willie Mitchell Boggs was not such a person. He was shot twice while he was attempting to rob a liquor store, but unfortunately he lived. One of the bullet wounds was a through-and-through type wound to the body, but unfortunately the injuries it inflicted were not fatal or even life-threatening. The second bullet broke his right arm. He would have been discharged from the charity hospital he laid in, had it not been for a rip-roaring infection that set up in his injured arm. On the third day his right arm had to be amputated right above the elbow. The day after the amputation, a deputy sheriff, who was also a cousin of Willie's, called from Galveston County. He was inquiring as to the amount of bond that had been set in Willie's robbery case. As soon as he was told about the amputation of his cousin's arm the deputy burst out laughing and wanted to know which arm. He went on to explain that Willie's father had been shot while pulling an armed robbery in Galveston County some twenty-five years before, and that he lost the same arm in the process.

Julio Saenz Jr. took up drug dealing to support a fast lane lifestyle. Nice clothes, nice cars, fast women, and parties do not come cheap. Julio was, however, stabbed to death in the garage apartment he rented from his grandmother in Houston's Cottage Grove subdivision. His mother was at the scene when the detectives arrived from the Central Station. She was adamant that her son was just a hard worker who just knew how to manage his money well. His killer would later confess that Julio would not extend him any credit on the cocaine he needed—so he killed him. An interesting aside to this urban renewal killing was that Julio's father had been killed twenty years to the day before Junior bought the farm. His murder also had been committed in the course of a drug deal.

These two sets of circumstances prove up one of two axioms. The first is *Who says gene polls don't breed true?* The second is that *You can't shine shit.* Both seem applicable.

FORTY-THREE

THE BANDIT WARS

The Bandidos motorcycle gang was founded by a scholar named Don Chambers in 1966. That gentleman would later die in prison. The group was composed of white trash (and some brown trash) bikers that banded together modeling themselves after California's Hell's Angels. With the political climate of the late 1960s and early 1970s the Bandidos fit in with the counterculture of the hippie/free love and drug movement. In all honesty they were just a group of petty low-rent drug-using criminals involved in burglaries, dope, prostitution and white slavery. They wanted the world to know that they were the baddest of the bad. The reputation they attempted to obtain was through violence and outlandish acts. One Houston motorcycle shop owner was badly beaten and many of his teeth were broken off with channel lock pliers while his girlfriend was sexually abused and tortured. This pretty well typified their feral human mindset and ways.

They ran (and continue to run) their girlfriends and wives in strip joints and the totally nude clubs. Most of these clubs were (and still are) nothing more than whorehouses on their best day anyway. At this point in time these gentlemen were nothing more than a loose-knit group of rag-tag criminals riding chopped up Frankenstein motorcycles built from multiple stolen bikes. As a sign of their being in charge they flaunted their badness by flying their colors.

The early part of the 1970s brought the concept of capitalism into the Bandits drug addled brains. They saw the Hell's Angels working security contracts at rock concerts using intimidation and brutality to keep rowdy concert goers in check. Then some companies in West Virginia and Tennessee hired local motorcycle gangs to ride shotgun (literally) on their trucks during labor union disputes.

The Bandidos began trying to flex their muscles in Houston in the early 1970s by taking over parts of town. They sought to take over the strip club industry by providing women, and hanging out at the clubs to intimidate the patrons and the club owners. One area of town that they sought to take over and stake their claim to was Downtown Houston's Old Market Square. At this point in history the Bandidos really wanted to proclaim themselves the Alpha Dogs of the motorcycle world. They swore allegiance to the Bandit Nation. Their lifestyle was a macho blend of motorcycles, drugs, guns and violence. It began to build to a head with acts of violence and confrontations with bar and business owners. Houston's then-chief of police was named Herman Short. He had brass balls, and when he walked they clanged. He ordered a crackdown on the Bandidos. All Bandits seen flying their colors were written five traffic citations and booked into the city jail. Their motorcycles were towed off on wreckers, many times hanging upside down. The scooter trash had been really pushing the envelope like school yard bullies with their outlandish behavior. Though it was never publicly acknowledged that a program had been instituted, the Bandits got hit from multiple sides at once. Houston's Tactical Squad of uniformed officers hit head-on with the biker trash downtown. These cops cracked heads and kicked ass with wild abandon, with flashlights, blackjacks and boots ruling the day.

The Pasadena Police brought on their own reign of terror that sought to humiliate the scooter trash and keep them low key inside their city. Any Bandit caught flying his colors in Pasadena was arrested for something—traffic tickets, littering—who knows what. When they were jailed their clothes were taken and they were dressed in jail jumpsuits. Then they were all sprayed for body lice and their clothes were washed in a 50/50 bleach and water solution for sanitation purposes. This included their beloved colors. It did not take long for these misguided children to learn to fight shy of Pasadena, Texas.

The Park Place station covered southeast Houston and those officers sought to rain havoc upon the misguided children whenever possible. The trashy bars and strip joints along Telephone Road and the Gulf Freeway were many times staffed by biker mommas. Biker trash in and around these clubs flying their colors went to jail for something. Some of these idiots were arrested for cause—some *just because*. The Southeast Station began a full court press that culminated in two large-scale shooting incidents. The first was the shooting up of a Bandido safe house in the Garden Villas subdivision. The second was the killing of three Bandido burglars during a sporting goods store burglary. The crooks were in the gun department when they were literally mowed down.

These two shooting incidents were followed by a full-blown street brawl between the night shift Vice Squad and a group of Bandidos outside a downtown coffee shop. The fight followed some tire-slashing incidents that had been occurring on the Vice Squad's cars in the downtown area. The Vice boys, along with a bunch of night shift detectives, had watering holes (clubs) that they frequented downtown. Many were on the north edge of downtown in the sector known as Old Market Square. There were several strip clubs in this area and

Vice had recently hammered several of them and jailed Bandido mommas with both liquor violation and prostitution charges. These poor women were forced to turned tricks at a high rate or some biker would beat the tar out of them or sell them off to some other bottom-feeding pimp. In the week following the titty-bar biker-whore roundups, no fewer than five Vice cars had their tires slashed. All of the vandalized cars were outside of downtown bars. No offense reports were ever generated and deals were cut with city wrecker drivers and tire shop employees and their supervisors. It is written somewhere that a couple of cases of confiscated whiskey at Christmas time can get a multitude of things accomplished in life.

The showdown with the bikers took place outside a twenty-four hour Greek-owned coffee shop named Annie's, off of Congress Avenue. After 11 p.m. Annie's was a place frequented by undercover and plainclothes cops, bikers, strippers, hookers as well as night people. It was a place where the cops and the street crud sat separately and was a sort of no-man's-land where the two classes of people ate and drank coffee but never interacted or mingled. After midnight the place took on an almost Holy Ground atmosphere where things were subdued and no real raucous behavior took place. You didn't want to get barred from the place because there wasn't another place to eat at that time of night for a pretty fair drive. That was until the night in question.

Five Vice cops and two Vice sergeants had been seated in Annie's for about three minutes when six Bandits rode up on their Harleys. The bikers sauntered in and one of them who called himself Bad Bob walked over to the cops' table. He had rude things to say about Robby Bostik's mother and her relationship with a German Shepherd dog. All of this was behind Bad Bob's old lady getting busted on two cases of liquor violations and a soliciting prostitution charge. Robby's only comment was, "Do you want to take this outside Faggot?"

Robby and Bad Bob walked quietly outside and every cop and biker in the place followed solemnly in a quiet procession. No words were exchanged and a beautiful fight ensued. No guns or knives were ever drawn. Two of the cops present habitually carried Convoy brand 15-ounce braided leather blackjacks, and neither was shy about the proper application thereof. After Robby kicked his opponent into oblivion he went and retrieved his 870 Remington shotgun from the trunk of his city car. The scattergun had an extended magazine and Robby ran it dry shooting up the bikers' motorcycles. When the shots began going off everybody scattered. No reports were ever made and nobody went to jail that night.

The federal government began getting into the Bandido-hunting business also and started having roundups of their own. Guns, dope and prostitution could be filed on the federal level too, which got the Bandits' attention. They took on a much lower profile and almost immediately got into the drug transportation business. They flourished financially to a great degree. Then with the incorporation of other motorcycle gangs into their ranks it caused a wholesale expansion and opening of drug trade and distribution routes. The individual members are still the lower forms of life they always have been. However they have done well financially because they were pressured and driven below the surface.

The hounding by police agencies brought them financial success and the ability to post bonds and hire high priced law firms. One Houston Bandido who called himself Sprocket had an interesting observation. Under the leadership of Chief of Police Lee Brown the practice of booking people on Class C misdemeanors and tickets stopped. He directed the police to write tickets for everything from theft under fifty dollars to urinating in public. Sprocket advised, "We ain't never had us no niggers in the Bandidos, but we're thinking about making Lee Brown an honorary member. He's kept more of us out of jail than any bondsman or team of lawyers ever could have."

On a lighter note—an interesting aside was the death of a Bandido named John Bachelor, alias Hang Around John. He died at the motorcycle drag races outside of

Porter, Texas in southern Montgomery County. John had not been out of prison long when he caused a confrontation with a member of the Banshees motorcycle gang. From the early days the Banshees and Bandidos have been rivals. The Banshees dwindled and the Bandit ranks swelled. Dear John came to his end after he pulled out a short-bladed sheath knife. He began to poke at a Banshee with it and threaten to cut the club rocker off his motorcycle jacket. The Banshee took offense to this action and produced a .25 automatic Titan semi-automatic pistol and center-punched Dear Johnny Boy.

Two-hundred-forty-eight-pound, six-foot-four Johnny Boy was dead on the ground within a few seconds from a single jacketed bullet. Many persons in the law enforcement community thought that the world was now a better place. A general fight broke out and several people were stabbed and/or assaulted. There would likely have been more deaths but two off-duty officers were present and broke up the melee by shooting their duty weapons into the ground. They said that in all honesty there was so much violence going in around them and knives and guns were very evident. They felt they were to be the next victims. That was their stated reason for cranking off a half dozen rounds.

The Montgomery County Sheriff's Department investigated the killing. They were not impressed by the dead man or any of the witnesses they could find. The off-duty deputies did not see the shooting, just the cutting and fighting that followed. The investigators were hard-pressed to find a credible or reliable person with no criminal history within the population they interviewed. The dead man just recently been paroled for an armed robbery conviction out of El Paso. They consulted with the Montgomery County District Attorney's Office who had very little interest regarding to the social signifi-cance of Mr. Batchelor's death.

The dead man was Houston trash, and not a local res-ident. As such the case was presented to a local small town grand jury and the passing of Saint John the Ban-dido was cleared as a *justifiable homicide.* Had the shooter been known, the ruling as to the shooting being justified would have been the same. The unusual part was the fact that an unknown and unnamed person unknown was cleared of any wrongdoing. Batchelor was armed with a knife (deemed a deadly weapon by law) with which he was prodding his killer. The unknown and never-to-be identified Banshee was cleared of any wrongdoing and no further action was ever taken by anyone other than to put the case on the shelf to gather dust. With the ruling being justifiable the murder was stricken from the coun-ty's crime statistics as if it never existed.

After John Batchelor met his just desserts the Bandits called a Council of War. They were discussing whether to take out a contract to kill more Banshees in retaliation for their loss. Contracts for such things are often taken out through other motorcycle gangs, and are a rather common practice. It is unknown to this author if more trash killings resulted from the passing of this mother's son.

The Bandidos now have chapters in all fifty states and several foreign countries. They have web pages where they sell ball caps and t-shirts, but they still are the same trashy people they have always been. They are social misfits who band together with like individuals. They are loyal only to their organization and would forsake their wives and children before their beloved Bandit Nation. In their case money can never buy them respectability. With motorcycles becoming a craze among upper class and upper middle class America, Yuppies now get exposed to the Bandidos from time to time. If they get too close they begin to see them for what they are. As a whole, the Bandits remain living proof that you can't shine shit and never could.

FORTY-FOUR

··

THE BIG LEG CONTEST

The Screaming Eagle was a nightclub in southeast Houston located east of Cullen Boulevard. To say the décor was unusual would be the understatement of the year. When you drove up into the parking lot the first thing you encountered was about twenty-five feet of jet airliner tail section sticking out of the parking lot's asphalt. When you entered the establishment you saw the cockpit and nose cone of a jet liner poking out of the wall above the main bar. There was no end to the multi-colored neon signs hanging all over the walls. There was a huge dance floor and stage. The color scheme and decorations could best be described as looking like they had been selected by a multitude of color blind pimps with an eye for anything gaudy and pseudo-Africanized in nature. The furnishings were not cheap, just tacky and very much overdone.

For several years if you were into the black nightclub scene in the southern part of Houston, the Screaming

Eagle was the place to go or to be seen. Friday and Saturday nights were the club's biggest dance and most active social nights during the week. During each week there was either a fundraiser or some contest or other. Another night there might be stand-up comics, a variety show or some sort of live entertainment. However, one of the most popular contests ever held during the week was billed by the management as The Best Legs in Houston contest.

This contest was, in fact, only held every other week. The lady that was judged to have the best legs that night was given a hundred dollar bill dollar as her prize and was given the chance to compete in the Best Legs of the Year contest. The Best Legs of the Year winner got a thousand dollars in cash and a red satin warm-up or baseball type jacket with white lettering showing the year she reigned supreme.

The judging began from bottom to top. In the black community, *big fine legs* are a highly lauded attribute on a woman. The judging of the contest was always conducted by the same three-man panel. It was a judging based upon their appreciation of horseflesh and confirmation as they saw it. All judging results were final and no rights of appeal were ever granted.

The women who were contestants in the bi-weekly contest were directed to stand upon a stage about five feet above floor level. The club's audience and the judges made their picks and culled the contestants in a three-tiered competition. The first one had the women hike their dresses up to knee level and turn, showing off their ankles and lower legs. The second had the ladies jack their skirts up to show their thighs and maybe some of their underwear. There was a disc jockey acting as the master of ceremonies introducing the ladies and keeping up a constant chatter. During this whole time the crowd and judges passed judgment on the race horses or pork chops that paraded before them. The third and final showing (as it were) consisted of the ladies either spinning about to show off their complete lower extremities, or removing their skirts completely to show their panties and posteriors. The wilder the contestant's clothing and undergarments that were exhibited the better the judges and competition watchers liked it. This contest (though it was officially called the Best Legs in Houston Contest) became known locally as the Big Leg Contest. You see beauty is in the eye of the beholder and big powerful legs and a rump like a quarter horse are definite assets in some neighborhoods.

All of the above listed information about this establishment and the Big Leg Contest has been passed along to lay out the predicate for the story that follows.

Late Thursday Night or Early Friday Morning

The 911 call dropped regarding an armed mentally ill woman holding her children hostage and threatening to kill them. Ushieka Kesterson called the police reporting that her daughter-in-law had called her just before midnight. Her distraught in-law reportedly told her that life was terrible and that it was no longer worth living. The truly disturbing news was when Tiffany said she was seriously considering "capping" herself and the rest of her family. Several police units responded along with a patrol supervisor and a crisis intervention unit. They all met a block away from the possible suspect's house in a school parking lot.

All of the parties involved were huddled in the parking lot formulating a game plan when the distraught woman's husband drove up. He asked his mother what was going on. She told him about his bride Tiffany calling her and that she had threatened to "cap" herself and take the rest of the family with her. David Kesterson busted out laughing and told his mother that was all bull corn and that Tiffany was just upset because she got eliminated on the second go-round from the Big Leg Contest at the Screaming Eagle earlier that very evening. The sergeant at the scene was named Jimmy Ray Priestly. Jimmy Ray was himself African-American and had been a patron of the club in question a time or two. Sergeant Priestly got on his cell phone and called Tiffany.

The audible portion of his side of the conversation went like this.

Ma'am, this is Sergeant Priestly with the Houston Police Department. You spoke with your mother-in-law Ushieka Kesterson earlier this evening and she is concerned about you. She called us out here to your house. She is concerned about your safety and that of your kids. Right now both Ushieka and your husband David are outside here talking with us. We need to clear this matter up right now.

I need for you to come outside and talk this over with us. I'm sure this whole thing is nothing but a big misunderstanding. What am I gonna do if you don't cooperate with us? Well first I'm gonna have my troops go up and down the street and wake up all of your neighbors and tell them not to get excited about all the police cars being outside. They'll tell them that you're just acting stupid 'cause you lost out early in the Big Leg contest at the Screaming Eagle tonight. Then I'm gonna enter your home and take you into custody and put you in a rubber room at the Harris County Psychiatric Hospital for three days. That's why I think it would be better for everyone if you just came outside and let us talk this thing out. If this whole matter is what I think it is then we will all very likely be going our separate ways in just a little bit. If you don't cooperate then there might be some reason for concern about your mental health. If so, I might have to revert to the earlier plan.

Miss Tiffany came outside directly. Sergeant Priestly made a mental note that this woman was no part of a beauty contestant. She said she had embarrassed herself very badly that night at the Screaming Eagle nightclub. She went on to say that she never would have gotten onto the stage if she hadn't been drinking those punch shooter drinks with her friends. She and her social group affectionately called the adult beverages in question Little Red Motherf***ers. Tiffany Kesterson went on and made the mistake of saying that life was no longer worth living. Though it was likely the booze she had consumed that was making the statement, Priestly was put into the position that the lady now needed to be taken into custody. She was transported to the Harris County Psychiatric Hospital for a court ordered 72-hour period of observation. Let them release her in a day or so. That way if she killed her kids it is on them not him.

Later while having breakfast with another sergeant, Jimmy Priestly wondered out loud why a double-wide warthog like Tiffany would enter herself into such a contest in the first place. Secondly he marveled that she made it through the first tier of the competition. He figured that in her case the elimination tool used in the second round of competition was a cat's-eye marble. "If you stuck a marble in a cellulite dimple and over half of it disappears then that person gets eliminated" he laughed. He closed that portion of the conversation with, "From what I could see it's all behind her now—or at least most of it was, anyway."

FORTY-FIVE

....

AN ELEPHANT GUN

Jennifer Lessor was not known to the police department prior to the day she started shooting her pistol and was, in turn, herself shot to death. For some unknown reason she began firing a handgun in the courtyard area of the apartment complex where she lived. The police were called out, as you might expect. Before their arrival she would, from time, to time step out of her apartment and fire a round or two before going back inside. The police arrived and walked up and knocked upon her door. She fired a round through that very door and the cops failed to see the humor in her actions. SWAT was called out to the scene. The Hostage Negotiation Team came out also.

One of the negotiators called her on the phone. She asked him if she were to step outside of her apartment's front door would he be able to see her. The officer responded that he would. The very heavy-set lady in question stepped outside wearing only a thin nightgown. She promptly mooned him, and anyone else who might be looking from the area of the street. Then she fired her handgun in the direction she thought he would be watching from.

Ms. Lessor then went back inside her apartment. She must have been watching the television from inside her apartment. It seems the local TV stations' helicopters were above the scene doing live broadcasting. The choppers' live broadcast showed the location of the SWAT team's brand-new Mobile Command Center and discussed it at length. The suspect first walked out of her back patio gate through a parking lot and onto a side street only one half block from the command post.

Jennifer (still barefooted and wearing a shear nightgown) walked approximately one hundred and fifty feet before opening fire on (and hitting) the new SWAT truck. Her movements had been noted and reported to the command post by a sniper on a nearby roof. He kept the C.P. advised right up to the point she opened fire upon the SWAT truck with her pistol. Just after she fired her first and only round at the truck, the sniper chest-shot the lady in question without hesitation. A street corner witness to the shooting related to a TV reporter that he saw the entire shooting and that, "First she raised up her gun and shot the one time at that big black truck and then he (the sniper) just dropped her like a bad habit." The marksman (in his statement) related that he was not going to allow the suspect to further endanger the lives of his co-workers and therefore he did not wait for authorization to shoot.

Homicide was, naturally, immediately called out to the scene. As usual prosecutors from the Civil Rights Section of the Harris County District Attorney's Office made the scene as well. One of the Homicide troops asked the Civil Rights section director. "Well Terry, what do you think about this one?" The crusty old prosecutor replied, "If nothing else, we have now been able to now establish one thing for certain. A Remington Model 700 rifle in .308 caliber can from now on be classified as being either an elephant gun or a walrus gun."

FORTY-SIX

....

THE 'QUE MAN

In the black community there exists a group of entre-preneurs that set up roadside stands in vacant lots and empty parking lots to sell barbeque. They do a brisk cash-only business on weekends, many times working only the evening and night time hours. Often much of their business is transacted between ten at night and three in the morning. The nightclub crowd likes to chow down after dancing and drinking, and the smell from the 'que pits can really pull them in like a fish on a string. These are unlicensed and uninspected operations be-cause the city health inspectors and tax collectors are headed home when these guys are just starting to set up shop. Some of these mobile establishments have quite a following and a regular clientele, and many of these street corner chefs can turn out some exceptionally good food products. The gentlemen that run these mobile food establishments are typically known in the hood as *The 'Que Man*. Because these guys are unlicensed and they are not inspected or regulated by the government, their table fare is at times uncharted. Sometimes wild rabbits or feral hog is on the menu, and at other times raccoon or possum may be served. Similarly, over the weekends dressed raccoons, possums and wild hogs may be sold at roadside meat markets, but that is another story. After the sun goes down or on weekends the normal rules of legal commerce may fail to apply in the Ghetto.

One such gentleman of color named Leander Fudge set up business in the parking lot of the La Chat Club on Old Spanish Trail just a few miles south of Houston's downtown area. He worked only on Friday and Saturday nights, but he would not work in the rain. His specialty was shredded barbequed raccoon sandwiches, and he sold out every night that he was open. During the week he ran his trap lines and skinned and froze the coons he would be cooking over the weekend. He would also cook a couple of briskets or chickens, which he usually sold after he ran out of his specialty meats.

The Fifteen District night shift officers out of the Beechnut station had a couple of country boy types. They would come on duty and race like hell for the La Chat Club to get their 'qued coon fix before the old man ran out. The 'Que Man cut the cops a half-price deal on his coon sandwiches. He knew after talking with them, that to those two Bohemian cops, barbequing was a puesdo-sexual out-of-body religious experience. It took second place only to beer consumption. If they could get a 'qued coon sandwich twice over the course of a week-end, the blue suits thought they were "crappin' in high cotton."

The La Chat 'Que Man had an odd operation, and how he kept from blowing himself to Kingdom Come is still anybody's guess. Leander had constructed his barbeque pit out of a 30-gallon metal drum. He took the trunk lid off of his aging Dodge compact car and set the drum in the bottom of the car trunk, right over the gas tank, and fired up his pit. The drum was chocked in place with a couple of bricks as he stoked it with some charcoal, but mostly with mesquite limbs. He made sure all his mesquite limbs had been allowed to air dry for at least 90 days before using the wood for cooking. His barbeque sauce simmered in a tin pan on the same end of the pit he kept the meat on. The fire was kept going on one end of the pit, and after the meat was cooked it sat on the opposite end of the pit from the smoking fire. Mister Fudge's greasy shredded raccoon meat sandwich-es with his brown sugar barbeque sauce had quite a fol-lowing. He had been a constant fixture in the La Chat parking lot for seven years when a junkie decided to try and rob him. Leander got so mad that he slapped the crooks knife aside and buried his 'que fork into the would-be bandit's side. The wanna-be jacker ran off holding his chitterlings and screaming.

The 'Que man jumped in his car and chased after Rodney Allen Ripoff as he ran screaming down the street. The old man jumped curbs and drove through lawns chasing the would-be armed robber. Witnesses related that a trail of fire and sparks could be seen coming out of his pit in his car trunk as he chased the wounded man through the neighborhood. The 'Que Man finally pinned the injured robbery suspect to an oak tree in somebody's front yard (using his front bumper). When the police arrived Leander was very highly concerned about how he was going to get his bone-handled turning fork back once it was removed from the junkie's guts.

Following Mister Fudge having to stab the robbery suspect he began openly carrying a short-barreled revolver in his hip pocket. He told the cops he had been carrying it under his shirt before but that he simply hadn't had time to get to it when he really needed it. He could legally carry the pistol because he was on private property and running a business sanctioned by the owners there. The weapon was a snub-nosed six-shot .38 revolver with the hammer spur cut off so it would not get hung up if he had to draw it. The dehorning of a revolver showed street survival skills on the part of the old man. Where he lived there was the quick and the dead, but rarely do you find many old fools.

FORTY-SEVEN

....

THE SPLASH BABY

Velveteen Nixon was a witness to a Sunday after-noon neighborhood shooting. It was simply a case where one neighbor shot another neighbor. Both men had been involved in a cuss fight and by all accounts they had pretty well exchanged an equal number of ver-bal slurs regarding incest with their respective mothers. Following the last exchange of MF salvos Darrell Wayne Roberson pulled out a pistol and shot his cuss fight op-ponent in both the chest and the tripe. Junior Boy Jones died at the scene. The offense changed from *disorderly conduct* to *murder* in a matter of only a few seconds.

Velveteen was a good witness and gave an exception-ally clear rendition of what transpired. The investigator who typed Ms. Nixon's affidavit had her sign her state-ment before a notary public that he called into his office. The notary was a female civilian and she asked the very pregnant witness when the baby was due and she was told "Any day." The female clerk then asked if the baby's daddy was excited about the upcoming birth and the answer came back as "Not really." Velveteen went on to explain that the baby's daddy was her sister's boyfriend. The notary was aghast and in disbelief said, "You were having sex with your sister's boyfriend?" The mom-to-be attempted to explain it all away with the following beyond-logic statement.

You see it was like this here. My sister and her boyfriend used my bed earlier in the day to mess around in. Later on when I got into bed to go to sleep some of it must have splashed on me.

The concept of a splash baby was quite novel and heretofore unknown to anyone in the Homicide office. Ms. Nixon was the only witness to the killing and who would come forward and tell the truth. The shooter refused to talk at all. Everyone involved in the case truly hoped their star witness would not repeat her splash baby story from the witness stand and thus blow her credibility all to Hades.

FORTY-EIGHT

....

THE TREE FELL

Rayfield Jeffers was not the sharpest pencil in the box. He had been a police officer fifteen years when he got promoted, and that was only on the coat tails of a discrimination law suit. He usually dictated his offense reports to a friendly clerical employee or two because when he tried to type, it was not very pretty. He was good at getting confessions out of prisoners and would at times call upon his white counterparts to play the *White Honky Racist Cracker* to get a prisoner to relate better to another brother man.

Ray-Ray took most of his confessions in a tape recorded mode because he could not spell worth a flip. His one attempt at typing a confession was so bad that when it was put into evidence at trial time Detective Jeffers had to read it into the record. The reason he had to read it aloud into the record was that nobody else could translate it into normal conversational English. The only words in it that were readily understandable were mother***er, and those alone did not tell much of a story.

The suspect, Hokey Simms, and his victim were both wino/street people. The suspect walked with a cane. He "juked" (stabbed) the victim multiple times after a drunken slur-filled verbal exchange. Simms first hit the dead man over the head with his walking stick and knocked him to the ground. He then pounced on his victim and stabbed him multiple times in the chest and abdomen. During the course of his stabbing frenzy Hokey cut himself badly on his left hand. It was very likely he was holding onto his victim and cut himself while monogramming the other man. Rayfield would testify that the defendant had been drinking but was not intoxicated. The truth was that he did not audiotape the confession because the suspect was so sloppy drunk that nobody could have understood his slurred speech. The following is a cleaned-up version of his typed confession—enabling normal folk to understand it.

Statement of Person in Custody

I, Hokey Sims, prior to the making of this statement, have been advised of the following rights by Sgt R.T. Jeffers.

1. I have the right to remain silent and not make any statement at all while I am in custody, and that any statement I make may and probably will be used against me at my trial.

2. I have the right to consult with an attorney prior to or during any questioning by police or agents of the state. If I am unable to employ a lawyer then one can be appointed for me free of charge.

3. I have the right to terminate this interview at any time.

4. I understand these rights, and I waive them and make this statement of my own free will.

This evening I was drinking under a big tree at the corner of Reed Road and Coffee Street. Junior Carmouche was there and he started messing with me and I told him to back off. Then he called me a useless paraplegic Motherf***er. That was when the tree fell on grandpa's hog. In the country that means all hell broke loose. First I whacked him over the head with my walking stick and it broke the second or third time I hit him.

I think I poked at him with my knife once or twice to keep him away from me. I've got a bad leg and I was afraid he was gonna hurt me. I somehow cut myself by accident so I went to the V8 (V.A.) hospital. I am not a veteran but I figured that if I went to the

county hospital I might get arrested for
juking (stabbing) Junior. It didn't work out
the way I planned and I am in Homicide giving this statement.

_____

Signature of Person Giving Statement

_____

Witness

_____

Witness

The above statement is a true and valid translation
from its original broken Ebonics and Ghetto Speak version into English.

FORTY-NINE

···

THE WRESTLING MATCHES

Joe Wilson was a patrolman with a total of one year's worth of seniority and he was riding the 3 p.m. to 11 p.m. shift out of the Central Station. It was a cold and rainy mid-February Saturday night and the nicest thing you could say about the weather was that it was miserable as Hell. There was nobody on the street and the radio traffic was so quiet that about every five minutes somebody was key their microphone just to see if their car radio was working. The lowest seniority officers on the shift usually get the oldest cars on the line. Joe's car showed in excess of one hundred thousand miles on the odometer, the driver's seat was broken down and the heater smelled like motor oil burning on a hot manifold. When a police car is put in use the motor will run every bit as long with the car sitting still as it does moving. So if a cop car shows a hundred thousand miles on its odometer, it has two hundred thousand worth of time on the motor. Wilson was looking for some reason to get out of the car and spend time elsewhere. If he had found someone to arrest he could spend time report writing and filing charges with the District Attorney's Office. No calls were dropping and the street animals were holed up out of the weather.

By seven o'clock that evening young Officer Wilson had enjoyed enough fun. He decided he would stop by the wrestling matches and visit with one of his trainers, an old-timer named Jimmy Ray "Smitty" Smith. Smitty worked a uniformed extra job at the wrestling matches downtown every Saturday night. It would be good to see Smitty again. It also might be good to be introduced to one of the Silicone Sisters that strut around the ring between rounds holding up placards for those people too stupid to know how to count the rounds.

Officer Joe Wilson was about to get a crash course into the wrestling industry. The rules dictate that hometown boys are the good guys and the out-of-towners are the low down skunks. When our local boys go on the road the roles are reversed and they become the no-goods. Wilson walked into the building just as the biggest and the baddest out-of-towner was making his way down the aisle and was approaching the ring. He was a truly massive man wearing black tights, no shirt and a leather mask. The crowd was booing and throwing popcorn bags and paper cups at him. The out-of-town bad-ass was playing it up for all it was worth. He was snarling and clawing at the air like a wild animal. Another thing that Joe did not know was that his old partner Smitty (though he was still wearing his police department's uniform) had now gotten into the production side of show business.

This out-of-town baddest-of-the-bad guy was so mean (according to the game plan) that he even fought with the cops before getting into the ring to battle some hometown hero. There was no way that Joe could have known that King Kong and Smitty had rehearsed and practiced their whole routine twice before the public was allowed inside the building that night. All Joe Wilson saw was a fifty-five-year-old Smitty Smith wrestling with a man twice his size. Next, the huge crazy man was trying to get Smitty's night stick away from him. Wilson rushed up and slugged the huge wrestler in the side of the head with his four cell flashlight, knocking the mammoth man to his knees. Then blood began to flow from the side of the wrestler's head like only a scalp wound can bleed.

Wilson reared back to finish off the masked monster with a second blow when, to his surprise, Smitty began to yell, "Joe—please stop! Dear God, you're gonna kill him!" It took both officers to get the injured wrestler up onto his feet. The crowd went wild with cheers and applause. The cops got the bloody wrestler into a rear dressing room and that is where Joe learned the truth.

Smitty was now part of the show and made an extra fifty dollars for fighting with a couple of out-of-town bad-asses. It was now part of an orchestrated act.

Nothing came from the head-busting incident. The World Wrestling Federation paid for the emergency room treatment and the medical follow-up care. The injured man was named Don Jordon and he and Smitty were long-time friends. Smitty, in fact, drove Don to the hospital in his personal car and stayed with him several hours while he was under observation. Joe was on national TV strumming the wrestler's head but nobody thought it was real so no Internal Affairs investigation took place. Don Jordon got six stitches and suffered a mild concussion. He was back on the national circuit two weeks later. To this day Joe Wilson will not even watch the wrestling matches on television.

....

FIFTY

THREE SHOOTING SCENARIOS

We live in a world of advancing technology and design in almost every field. This includes firearms and their projectiles. SuperVel began the ammunition revolution with their high velocity hollow-point ammunition in the early 1970s. There has since been continued improvement and experimentation in the development of expanding defense type ammunition. The quality in that industry has become superb. Similarly, firearms had come along way also. Police sidearms transitioned from revolvers into highly reliable semi-automatic handguns. Pistol sights became better and then night sights became common to assist both law enforcement and the general public in defending themselves. These improvements in working tools are all fine and good, but first and foremost you must always keep in mind that there are no guarantees in life. When you live in a world of whack-jobs and dopers there is always a good probability that Murphy may be hiding around the next corner.

Here are three stories of shooting situations where men I rode with in a patrol car were involved. Interestingly enough these were not the first on-duty shooting any of these men had been involved in.

Charlie Hull

Charlie Hull was riding a one-man day shift patrol unit. He responded to a 911 emergency call regarding a mental case attempting to break into a doctor's office on Hillcrest Street. The suspect in that case (Roger Coleson) was, in fact, attempting to chop his way through the front door of the business with a double-bitted axe. Charlie pulled up within forty-five feet of the business' front door. He observed the mental case actually making kindling out of the business' two-inch thick oak front door in his attempt to get to his estranged wife. Officer Hull advised the dispatcher of the situation and bumped the siren on his patrol car to get the nut case's attention. He got it all right. Coleson changed his focus from an oak door to a café-au-lait colored cop.

The nut case raised his axe over his head and went after the lone officer. Charlie called out once for the man to stop and then put the front blade of his Colt Government Model in the middle of the man's chest before he started firing. Roger Coleson showed no response to reaction to the gunshots. Hull fired again and again and again. Roger never stopped coming at him.

Charlie had been a military policeman in the Army and was weaned on a .45 Colt. He was watching his front sight and knew that there was no way in Hell that he was not hitting this 200-pound six-foot-tall target. Roger Coleson kept coming and soaked up a total of eight rounds of good quality hollow-point ammunition before he dropped dead at the officer's feet.

The ambulance that was called to the scene to attend to the very dead mental case wound up hauling Officer Hull to the emergency room. Charlie Hull's blood pressure spiked to Plus P stroke levels and would not go down for an extended time. Following the period of extended high blood pressure Charlie Hull began experiencing kidney failure. He did not respond to treatment with medication, so he had to begin dialysis treatments. Thirteen months later, Charlie Hull died while awaiting a kidney transplant. Roger Coleson did, in fact, kill his man. It just took him longer to do so.

Lawrence

Thomas Lawrence also rode the day shift out of the Southwest Station. He was a good troop who answered his radio and was not out to prove anything. He had over twenty years in uniformed patrol and did not shirk his duties. He responded to a *suspicious male* call in a strip shopping center on Fondren Road on the Harris and Fort Bend county lines. The suspect was a Hispanic male and the clothing description on the call slip identified him down to his tangerine-colored boots.

The suspect (Julio Mata) was drunk at eight thirty in the morning and in no mood to talk with a cop. His blood-alcohol level would later be determined to be .018. In police language he was twice drunk. The suspect first tried the "No hablo Ingles" routine. The officer then began questioning him in Spanish but he was not responsive to Tom's questions. Then Mata just chose to ignore the officer's demand of identification and failed to answer any questions asked of him. Lawrence called for a backup unit and told the drunken man to have a seat on the curb and put his hands on his knees.

Mata was not going to do what he was told. Julio put his hands up in front of him and told the blue suit "Okay-Okay." The laborer reacted as quickly as a cat. He stepped forward and shoved the officer down and sprinted away through the parking lot. Tom religiously worked out with weights and was both a runner and a motocross enthusiast. He took off on foot after the combative drunk. The officer did not want the drunk to get to his vehicle both for his own safety and that of any citizen. The good officer said his first concern was that Stupid would chose to drive off at a high rate of speed. Lawrence's own mother had been crippled for life a couple of years earlier by a drunk driver, so he understood the potential danger there.

The drunk ran up to a black Chevy pickup. To the officer's surprise, instead of jumping inside the vehicle, Macho Man pulled a 9mm Ruger pistol out of the driver's door map pocket. Mata was bringing his gun to bear on the officer when the still-running Tom Lawrence reacted with a smooth draw and performed a one-handed, double-tap (fire two rounds) motion. Julio then fired back but missed at a distance of about fifteen feet. The officer sought cover behind a parked car and the pissed-off drunk began walking toward him, continuing to as he advanced. Tom put his front sight on the suspect's chest and continued firing.

The cop later said that he felt sure he had to be hitting the suspect, but the 200-grain CCI hollow cavity bullets were not even slowing the man down at all. The 5'8"-tall, 155-pound man showed no reaction other than his obvious determination to kill the officer.

Rounds were hitting the car all around officer Lawrence. After his last double tap, the slide locked on his now empty .45 Colt. Tom knew to break and run to another location. He sought more cover and was reloading as he moved. The rattled officer sought cover on the off side of a Ford F250's engine block and began directing more .45 slugs at the man who was trying to kill him. One of this last group of rounds hit the suspect's pistol. Julio stopped and began trying to clear the jam the bullet had caused. Lawrence fired once more and the suspect dropped flat on his back. The last round he fired parted the suspect's mustache perfectly right below his nose. The bullet exited the back of Julio's head and the would-be cop killer was fully rehabilitated.

Julio Mata sustained gunshot wounds to his right upper leg and to both the left and right sides of his abdomen. What is more, both of his arms had been broken but it did not slow him down or keep him from trying to clear his jammed pistol. He was feeling no pain and was mad at the world.

The suspect's truck yielded a length of rope, one pair of handcuffs, a filet knife, a plastic tarp and two rolls of duct tape. It is thought he was going to try and abduct his estranged wife, but that is just supposition. What is known was that the wanna-be cop killer had absorbed enough foot pounds of energy to drop a Brahma bull but he had showed no reaction. It just goes to show that there are no silver bullets in life that will stop the were-wolf every time without fail.

Cracker

Michael "Cracker" Leverge was a night shift officer out of the Beechnut Station in southwest Houston. He was a college-educated aggressive officer who hailed from the good old boy Dixie south. His shifts were spent looking for criminal activity and putting dirt bags in jail. If you are working the midnight shift and are aggressively seeking criminals, your chances of getting into a shooting situation increases geometrically rather than numerically.

Mike attempted to stop a speeding Porsche one Sunday morning about three, and was led on a ten-minute chase southbound on the Southwest Freeway. The driver hit a curb after he exited the freeway and was attempting to make a U-turn under the freeway. When he did so, he blew out a tire. The dispatcher had already relayed the information along to Cracker that the car he was after had been taken the night before in a carjacking situation. After Lamont Jenkins' right front tire blew, he jumped a curb and the right front wheel literally folded up underneath the expensive play toy. The suspect's car slid up into a vacant parking lot. Lamont stepped from the expensive Quiche-Car clad in a designer suit and brandishing a nickel- and gold-plated .45 Colt. Michael bailed out with his trusty 870 Remington 12-gauge in hand. Jenkins swung around and faced Mike Leverge, pointing his .45 at the lanky cop.

The 870 riot gun began belching fire and Number 4 buckshot pellets began punching holes in Lemont's fancy clothes. The problem was, however, even though the crook had been shot, he remained on his feet. Again and again the pump gun fired and the dapper carjacker stayed on his feet. Jenkins also retained his pistol in his right hand and repeatedly attempted to bring it to bear upon the uniformed cop. An overhead news helicopter recorded the whole thing. There were a total of five rounds of buckshot that were fired at Lamont that night.

Four of those shot patterns impacted the gunman's body and the fifth displayed itself nicely on the side of the wrecked sports car. Three rounds hit the suspect before he fell onto his back. He then sat up and pointed his pistol at Mike Leverge once more. Mike was coming around the back of his car and he fired a fourth time and missed, hitting the car. His fifth round of buckshot put the suspect down for good and the crook's handgun clattered to the pavement.

The suspect was hauled off to Ben Taub hospital where he lived four more hours at taxpayers' expense. The Homicide detective that made the hospital investigation was named Dale Ashton and he laughed when he saw the x-rays. Lamont had buckshot pellets in his head, feet, and all points in between. "Those x-rays made it look like that stupid bastard has the measles" he later proclaimed, to the entertainment of everyone in the squad room.

Two side notes to this case should be noted. Lamont Jenkins was a shooter and his weapon would later be ballistically linked to two other shooting scenes. His .45 was carried in a locked-and-cocked mode. He kept a hollow-point in the chamber and ball ammo in the magazine. It appears that Mike just didn't give the suspect enough time to shoot at him. Officer Mike Leverge still carries an 870 Remington shotgun, but he now loads it full of oo buckshot. It will now give him adequate penetration to turn the lights off much earlier in the game. He also has become a true believer in the one-ounce rifled slug: *Hallelujah and Amen Brother.*

The suspect's autopsy showed that the armed felon had been loaded up on cocaine at the time of his death. There is one axiom that holds true through each of these shootings. When someone is feeling no pain you must hit them with something heavy enough to shut down the central nervous system.

Praise the Lord and pass the ammunition.

FIFTY-ONE

....

THROW-DOWNS

The term throw-down relates to a gun or knife that is planted at the scene of a bad or unjustified police shooting. In other parts of the country such a thing might be called a throwaway. The word stems from the concept of just throwing a weapon down beside the dead body to justify how the dead person got that way. It is a police term that was in Houston pretty much was unknown outside the law enforcement community until the use of two such weapons (guns) were discovered. Both shootings took place in southeast Houston and the fact that the weapons were throw-downs was discovered during the course of follow-up investigations. Several officers' lives were ruined over two pieces of human garbage that were not really worth the effort. The cost to the officers' families can never be calculated. Children grew up without fathers present and without adequate financial support, and all of it for no good reason.

In fact, both of the aforementioned cases were justifiable shootings, but the officers chose to try and fabricate evidence rather than tell the truth and explain their actions. In all honesty, at that time in history you did as you were directed. The police department's rank and file at the time was at odds with both the mayor and the chief of police. That chief would later go to prison for corruption. It seemed to the line officers that they were more at risk from the city's upper management than from the crooks. It was an *us-against-them* mentality that prevailed at the time. When a senior officer or sergeant told you how something happened, you followed his lead and you stuck with your story.

One of the cases was an accidental discharge following a high-speed chase with a stolen van. That chase had reached speeds of over one hundred miles an hour. The stolen van spun out and an officer approached the driver's door with his duty weapon drawn. The suspect bailed out of the van and the closest officer to him grabbed the unarmed suspect with one hand and struck him once in the head with his pistol while trying to subdue him. At that point in history, striking someone with your pistol was not uncommon for the police to do. Nightsticks were not yet issued by the department and the carrying of blackjacks, or slappers, was permitted, if not openly encouraged. When that specific cop struck the suspect in the head with his pistol it bent the officer's gun's aluminum trigger guard and accidentally discharged. The young suspect died immediately from an unintended gunshot wound to his head.

Rather than simply tell the facts as they occurred, a throw-down of unknown origin and heritage was produced and placed near the body. The gun had unfortunately been used in a suicide some years earlier and it had somehow walked off from the police property room. The officer that produced the weapon for use that night would later testify he found it in a patrol car's glove compartment and kept it for a throw down. The officer who shot the felon was justified in having his pistol out and in his hand. The suspect was attempting to get away and the officer struck him with his pistol in an attempt to subdue him. Unfortunately the double-action semi-automatic weapon discharged and a death resulted.

The second throw-down case that brought the term to the forefront again involved the high-speed chase of a *burglary of a motor vehicle* suspect. That suspect was seen by multiple non-police witnesses to be shooting at the officers as they chased him over a twenty-mile stretch of freeway. It was a running gun battle that ended in a crash and the fatal shooting of the suspect/driver. There was no gun found at the scene. Unfortunately, someone produced one to be dropped inside the car. An ATF check on the weapon showed it had been purchased originally by a Houston officer who died from a heart attack well over a year before the shooting in question. Again, things went to Hades in hurry.

Several good men went to prison when the simple truth would have cleared everyone. The federal *conspiracy to commit* statute in the United States Code will convict you if you are in the same state at the time of the alleged offense. Some United States attorneys will, in fact, withhold evidence. They are from your federal government, and damned sure are *not* always here to help you.

If someone were to procure a throw-down it would be best if it were manufactured well prior to 1968. This is the year that sales records were mandated by the 1968 Gun Control Act, passed following the assassination of President Kennedy. The gun alleged to be the murder weapon in Kennedy's assassination was purchased via mail order. The new federal law required the keeping of sales records by gun dealers. These records contain detailed information about each buyer, such as driver's license and social security numbers.

The following story regarding a throw-down came from either Houston's north side or San Antonio's south side, depending who is telling it. A nighttime burglar was rehabilitated inside a high school by means of a couple of loads of buckshot. The first got his attention while he was standing and the second struck home as he reclined upon the school's floor. After a thorough search of the premises for additional suspects, a .22-caliber throw-down pistol was dropped beside the body. It hit the floor only after a good wiping down with a slightly oily rag.

To the officers' dismay the Saturday Night Special fell on its hammer as it hit the floor and discharged into the cadaver's leg. The handgun in question was made of pot metal and its hammer spur broke off after it hit the concrete floor. The shooter claimed he saw the suspect brandishing a handgun just before he was forced to fire upon him in self-defense. Both uniformed cops noted in their statements that they heard a light-caliber weapon discharge between the first and second shotgun blast.

Eighteen .32-caliber shotgun pellets and one .22-caliber slug were recovered by an overworked Harris (or Bexar) County Pathologist. For the officers' sake, they were lucky that tissue samples were not taken from around the .22-caliber entry wound in the dead man's leg. That way, it was never checked to see if any of the injuries were inflicted upon the dearly departed either pre- or post-mortem. There again all stories get better with the telling. Quen Sabe?

Some agencies in Texas follow and use the state's penal code regarding what is allowed in the use of deadly force by their officers or deputies. Other agencies restrict the use of deadly force far closer and do not allow killing people strictly because they are burglars or are in the course of committing a theft at night. Who is to say which is best for society? Rehabilitation can be brought about following several types of treatment, some clinical, some post mortem, and some post ass-whipping.

FIFTY-TWO

TOMMY T.

Tommy Tish was a pimp, gun runner and hustler. He would run whores, transport dope or guns, and shoot or beat up people for money. He would even let you make the choice as to whether you wanted somebody shot and wounded, shot and killed, simply beaten badly enough to get their attention or beaten to death. It was the customer's call. Different situations call for differing tactics. You see, dead men can't pay the money that they owe you. The man in question stood 6'2" and weighed in at 210. He was a pug-nosed killer who loved flashy things. He spoke good Spanish and had many connections in both Nuevo Laredo and Monterrey, Mexico. If he made a promise he would stand by it, even if it cost him money. The Houston headquarters for this former Pasadena, Texas native was the Vagabond Motel and nightclub on Houston's North Freeway. His girls did not rob people and they were checked weekly for communicable diseases. Business was business. If you did not pay one his girls for services rendered he would also take it out of your hide in spades. It was a matter of principal. You see, if he were to let someone beat him out of money then his reputation would suffer. He did not hold out money on his girls and they got their nightly 60/40 cut for the services they'd rendered.

Tommy had, at one time, been the manager of a top-less club called the My Office Club in Corpus Christi, Texas. After he left that job he continued to frequent high-end strip clubs and fancy restaurants. Tish had a steadfast rule that the ladies in his stable were not allowed to date blacks. This rule was in place to try and keep the black pimps away from his girls. You see, pimps are always trying to steal from one another. Tommy also felt that his high-rolling white customers did not want to spend money on women that had relations with black men.

One night in the nightclub at The Vagabond, a flashy dressed black male was standing around the club visiting with one of Tom's working girls. The man was advised by Tommy that he did not allow his girls to date black men and he told the gentleman in question to just to move along and leave the lady alone. In about a half hour's time the very same lady and gentleman in question walked outside of the club and got into a car. When Homeboy got behind the wheel, our Northside pimp in question walked up to the Cadillac and knocked on the driver's window. Homey rolled it down and Tommy said, "I told you to leave her alone." The killer took one step back and then fired a single round into the man's left temple from his pornographic .45 Colt. The lady in question began screaming and acting hysterical after she was splattered with blood and brain matter.

Tommy Tish then walked over to his Gentleman Jim custom pickup truck and put his favorite weapon under its front seat. He next pulled a six-pack of beer from the cooler that he kept on the truck's passenger side front floorboards. Then he sat himself on the tailgate of his fancy pickup. The hysterical woman was brought over to his pickup and he sat her down with him and they each had a beer. She and the club's Hispanic doorman joined Tom as they waited for the paramedics and then the police to arrive. The two witnesses to Homey's killing advised the police (and later gave sworn statements to the effect) that they had seen two Hispanic males run up to the car. One of the men demanded Homegrown's money and then he shot Homey in the head. The crooks then ran off. The doorman didn't get a good look at the suspects but simply heard the shot and saw two men run off. He could give little more than a clothing description and a direction of travel. The man with the gun was said to have a moustache and the other guy was thought to be clean-shaven. The two witnesses both gave a somewhat similar clothing description.

This killer of much repute was an odd sort. He was clean and always well dressed. He was not argumentative, nor did he curse or use bad language very often. He was a man of action and threats were not his style. One night in a Houston ice house, Tom got into a pool game with a member of the Bandidos motorcycle gang. The Bandit was a massive guy who always wore sleeveless shirts and he had a reputation for being a bad-ass. Muscle Man was said to have possibly been a professional wrestler at one point in his life and obviously pumped a lot of iron. The biker swaggered around and obviously thrived on intimidating people. The men were shooting a game of pool for twenty dollars. Tommy won and told the man to pay up. Mister Macho bellowed at the winner of the game, "I'll whip your ass before I'll give you a damn dime!" Tommy stroked the man twice in the head with the butt of the pool cue before that gentleman hit the floor. Then Mr. T kicked both of the man's kidneys enough times to ensure that himself would be passing blood in his urine for a week.

Following this exhibition of fast and effective brawling Tom removed the man's wallet and retrieved the twenty dollars he was owed. The wallet was then replaced. The Bandit at this point was lying on his side. Tommy then unbuckled the biker's jeans and proceeded to pull the man's pants and underwear down to his knees. Tommy then told the other club patrons, "When he comes to, I want you to tell him that I only f***ed him up this time. If he every crosses me again I will f*** him for real."

The money was not the real reason for the display of speed and savagery that shocked even the hardened group of patrons in the beer joint that night. It was a matter of reputation protection that brought on these acts. He could not allow it to be known that someone had backed him down and cheated him out of money that was rightfully his. In doing what he did, he also saved himself a lot of future problems. After the word got around about what he'd done to the monster biker over a twenty dollar bet, even fewer people would want to take the chance of crossing him. There was likely another motive for his actions. You see, the Bandidos have, for a long time, run some of their women in the strip clubs and pimped them through both the high- and low-end operations. With the word getting around about him not being afraid to take down a man of reputation, other pimps (of which some Bandidos are) would stay away from his stable.

Mr. T was alleged in a four-count federal indictment handed down out of New Orleans, Louisiana to be a high-ranking member of the infamous "Camarat family" headquartered out of Houston. The family in question was run by one Sam Camarat who owned a nightclub of his own in Houston. The indictment alleged six separate murders in which the eleven men charged were responsible. Also included in the indictment were charges of *racketeering, conspiracy to transport marijuana and cocaine, murder* and *conspiracy to commit murder*. Tommy was alleged by the U.S. Marshal's Service to be the family enforcer for the Camarat clan. Further, he was alleged to have been responsible for three of the six murders alluded to in the indictment.

Tish disappeared while out on a five hundred thousand dollar bond on these federal charges. He left several suicide notes. His former employer and the alleged head of a criminal drug operation, Sam Camarat, was sentenced to forty-five years for marijuana and cocaine distribution, conspiracy and a RICO (engaging in organized crime) racketeering charge. The crime operation was supposed to have operated out of Mexico and Colombia and the distribution system was spread among Texas, California, and Colorado. Crooks know that a federal *conspiracy to commit* charge is almost impossible to beat in court. The crooks and defense attorneys both will tell you that if you are alive and in the same state where the alleged acts took place you will be found guilty. The odds are always heavily stacked in favor of the prosecution and you are almost certain to be found guilty. Any criminal defense attorney worth his salt will advise his clients of this hard and fast rule of life. This is the basis for the expression, "Whatcha gonna do, make a federal case out of it?" Many of your civil rights are glossed over in the process. It takes a whole lot less to prove up a conspiracy charge in federal court than it does in state court.

Tommy was hiding out in Mexico at the time of his death. The Feds had warrants out for his arrest for a violation of the RICO (racketeering and organized crime) statutes where they alleged a narcotics conspiracy and at least six murders. He was out on bond and but failed to appear for trial. There were wanted posters all over Houston, Corpus Christi and New Orleans with a cash bounty that had been posted on his head like a coyote. To say the man was as hot as a two-dollar pistol is an understatement. There were cops and bounty hunters jacking up people that even remotely looked like him in either a clean-shaven or bearded condition. His death was officially listed in the civil registry in the city of Jalapa, in the state of Vera Cruz as being due to complications arising from surgery on his back. Some of the Vera Cruz civil servants also advised that he died during surgery on his sinuses.

Word of Tommy's death got to his former Houston roommate, Sonny, almost immediately. Sonny's wife loaded up and crossed into Mexico and retrieved the body. The lady knew that it was difficult to get bodies out of Mexico for burial in the States. She drove to the border and at Brownsville stopped in customs and advised the border agents there that she had the remains of one of the ten most wanted men in America in the back of her station wagon. Upon notification of Mr. T's death, a Texas Ranger and an FBI agent hustled to Matamoras, Mexico to photograph and fingerprint the cadaver before it was shipped to family in the States. It was not a pretty sight, in as much as embalming is not practiced in sunny Mexico. The body had cotton balls stuffed up its nose. It also showed obvious burn marks on the man's chest. It appeared that red hot loops made from a coat hanger type wire had been laid on his skin while he was being tortured and most likely questioned about something. The Texas Ranger who traveled down south knew Tish by sight. He was joined by an FBI agent and a member of the Texas Department of Public Safety's Criminal Intelligence Division. They photographed and fingerprinted the body so there would never be any question about the identity of the cadaver.

During the course of fingerprinting the cadaver it was rolled over onto its side and a round hole (probably .38 or 9mm in diameter) was located well centered in the dead man's back. There was also obvious powder stippling noted in the photographs around that bullet's entry hole. This indicated a close or loose contact type gunshot wound. Had the gun been shoved up against the body it would have left a star shaped mark where the muzzle blast would have cut the skin in a telltale pattern.

Also noted was a line of stitches on the outside of his left arm, as if a doctor had closed a wound of unknown origin.

It is often said in police work that "truth is often the first casualty, followed by the party who begins to assume room temperature." There were rumors that Tommy had been negotiating with the U.S. Attorney's Office for immunity from prosecution and placement into the Witness Protection Program. Another story told of how he was shot and wounded while fleeing from a contract killing in Mexico. He allegedly had just completed the contract killing of a Mexican general's son and was wounded in the arm trying to escape. Life in prison would have held no appeal for our boy either way. He was a flamboyantly trashy, flashy and very vicious individual. However, if he liked you he was your friend and would stand by you. Upon his death there was a multitude of Northside Houston turds that breathed a collective sigh of relief. FBI agents, city cops, and county cops of all flavors were jacking up every dark-haired and bearded man with a pug nose they could find. Some of his previous business associates similarly breathed easier when the news of his demise reached them. They'd also heard the Feds were looking to play *let's make a deal* with Tommy like they had with Sammy the Bull out of Chicago. In fact, the company that had to stand good on his half a million surety bond was quoted in the Corpus

Christi paper as saying that they had information that Tommy had become a government informant. Those that knew him very well contend that the bonding company was trying to get even with Tommy by putting out that he was turning snitch. They will tell you (that in his world) that Mr. T was a man of principle, no matter how skewed those principles might have been. The truth was that he would not have been of any use to the prosecution. Everybody in his drug operation group had already been convicted and was in prison by the time that allegation was printed in the Corpus Christi papers. Tom had been a Corpus Christi resident for a pretty good while before the Feds leveled the RICO charges against him, and he would only return to Houston for business dealings.

Tommy's favorite weapon of all time was a highly engraved and gold inlaid satin nickel plated 70 Series Colt Government Model. It was equipped with ivory grips that were highly scrimshawed with dramatically pornographic scenes. The ladies in the gold inlay on the top of the .45's slide were spread-eagle and lying upon their backs. No detail of their anatomy was left out or unseen. Tommy called it his *four-point sighting radius*. The weapon in question was sold by Tommy to the weapon's current owner in order to obtain quick cash to post bond on a charge approximately seven years before he came to his death. He sold it then because he needed bond money on a charge of having an underage girl working in his stable. That weapon is part of an extensive .45 collection owned by a Mr. Gus Cargile (actual name) of Corpus Christi, Texas. It is on display along with a photo of Tommy in his coffin with the burn marks on his chest and cotton balls up his nose. Just before Tommy jumped bond the weapon's former owner told Mr. Cargile that he'd killed around twelve men with that specific weapon. However he could only remember seven or eight of their names. He promised to write down the names so the gun's current owner could someday research the cities and names. Our boy disappeared shortly thereafter and never resurfaced alive.

The gunsmith who worked on Tommy's weapons advised that he had replaced parts of the .45 in question a multitude of times. It seems that from time to time Tommy would call the pistol smith and make an appointment to have his weapon "overhauled." The barrel, firing pin, ejector and extractor would each be replaced and the breach face around the firing pin hole would be polished with very fine emery paper. The man who Mr. T chose to work on his favorite handgun said he did this around ten or twelve times to that specific Colt pistol. He also said that his colorful client would also always take the old parts he'd replaced with him when he left the shop.

An aside about the weapon is that while it was being engraved, Tommy stopped by the engraver's shop wanting his weapon back. The engraver told him that the job had not been completed. Tommy reportedly told him, "Just give it to me. I need it right now, and I will bring it back to you shortly." Within two hours the gun was said to be back in the shop, needing cleaning but it had been returned so the engraving job could be completed. Another interesting point regarding this weapon is observed on the front end of the slide. The top of the barrel bushing bears the legend *Welcome to Hell* engraved so you can see it only if you are looking down the pistol's barrel. Tommy always loaded his .45 with the first round being a hollow-point followed by seven fresh rounds of ball ammo. He liked the job that 200-grain CCI hollow cavity bullets did, but he lived on the reliability of hard ball ammo.

When Tommy T. died, the Harris County Hospital District and the Harris County Morgue saved a substantial amount of money. The end result was that a whole lot less knee-capping, pistol-whipping and killing took place throughout Texas for several years to come. The names in this story have been modified slightly, but not to protect the innocent. One of the alias names Tommy had been known by was, in fact, Tish. His former employer's last name was almost Camarat. A lot of documentation exists on Tom's charges, his failure to appear and the information that was floating around that he had possibly turned informant. A true crime book could be written about Tom and his employer Sam Camarat. Tommy Tish was, in fact, a very interesting case study.

There have been multiple characters over the years that have told me of Tommy was connected to many high profile murders throughout Texas. They however would never say how they knew, or give statements or depositions as to how they knew this was true. Tom was also linked to a high profile killer out of Huntsville who also seemingly had nine lives. They were alleged to have killed people who generally just disappeared. Some of their victims were found floating in both Galveston and Corpus Christi Bays, in order to make a statement. One man with some very high-powered politically-placed family members was found floating inside a 55-gallon drum in Corpus Christi Bay. The three men reportedly involved in that killing learned that simply poking holes in the drum alone would not cause it to sink permanently.

As bodies decompose they will float due to gases building up in the body cavity. The actual cavity itself needs to be opened to let the gases escape. The killers would later determine that a minimum of two hundred pounds of cement needed to be added and the body cavity needed to be vented to complete the disposal formula. All tradesmen become more proficient with years of practice.

Those three gentlemen got a lot of practice. Two of these three killers are now dead. The third will be rotting inside a federal prison for the rest of his natural life. All of the aforementioned men understood one hard-and-fast rule. Death and/or prison are simply the cost of doing business when you choose certain vocations or paths in life. For he who lives by the sword shall die by the sword. Tommy Tish, however, would have told you that it was not the earth that the meek shall inherit—but rather the dirt.

FIFTY-THREE

....

TWICE DEAD

In most counties in Texas people are pronounced dead by a politician called a Justice of the Peace. He or she will also list the cause of death on the death certificate. The J.P. further is charged with determining if they should authorize a body to be transported to a medical examiner's office for autopsy. Autopsies are required by Texas law under certain circumstances—particularly in violent deaths or murders.

Regarding the causes of death, the county really does not want to pay for an autopsy if there is any way that they can get out of it. Many times the justice of the peace attempts to make an educated guess. Some are educated guesses that come about after interviewing family members or family doctors to see if there was a history of past medical problems. Some rulings are made by some odd methods that some former plow jockey has put together by means of some cockeyed logic cooked up within his pea brain. One J.P. used to rule a death to be a heart attack when someone was found lying face down. Similarly he ruled deaths to be caused by a stroke when bodies were found lying on their backs.

If you are related to a justice of the peace or to someone in the county with political clout, then suicides can become accidental deaths or murders. That way, life insurance policies pay off even if they are within their two-year contestable period. In Texas, insurance companies must pay off not matter what the circumstances if the policy has been in force for two years. That is, unless it states otherwise in the terms of your contract. An example of which might be that the company will not pay the face value of the policy if the dead person was in the commission of a felony at the time of their death. Double indemnity clauses don't pay off in the case of suicides either, but accidents are a whole different thing. One case in far south Texas was ruled a suicide even though the victim was shot in the back seven times with a .22-caliber bolt action rifle. That ruling was made by a medical examiner and pathologist whose cause of death rulings were often suspected to be for sale for many decades thereafter. That doctor died of natural causes recently and is hopefully burning in Hell at this very time.

Once upon a time in a land north of Houston and among the pine trees there lived a family of professional alcoholics. Their family name was Steele. The patriarch of that clan was a one-armed ex-con named Blue. Now Blue Steele was as vile an individual as anyone could ever get downwind of. If he were to have ever bathed he would likely lose several pounds. Cops hated to make calls when Blue passed out somewhere. He was bad enough to deal with when he was up and mobile. When he passed out and puked (or worse) upon himself you really didn't want to touch him or put him in your patrol car.

On several occasions the pungent Mister Steele had been staggering around with a bottle in his hand when he chose to pass out. On two of those occasions he cut himself badly and everyone thought he'd bled to death. The first time it occurred all over a roadway and the second time a parking lot. He was so nasty nobody really wanted to touch him. On both instances the responding paramedics had not been able to see any respiration and he had lost quite a bit of blood. Rather than check his vital signs he was pronounced dead by means of a long-distance visual check.

The justice of the peace was called out, but she didn't like to be in close proximity to dead bodies anyway. She would ask some paramedic or law enforcement officer "Is he (or she) dead?" If they responded "Yes ma'am, he (or she) is dead" then she would make her declaration as to the cause of death and advise the funeral home coach at the scene where to take the body. She would then tell the policeman of sheriff's deputy that brought her out (on night time death declarations) to take her home. The second time she pronounced Blue Steele to be dead he awoke on the prep table at the black funeral home. He did so while two employees therein were stripping the nasty clothes off his scrawny carcass. The attendant closest to old Blue that night ran completely through the back screen door without bothering to stop and unlatch it first.

It is unknown if living under pine trees causes people to act in such a manner. Blue Steele did, in fact, die an accidental death. He was even somewhat close to sober when he was hit by a major freight carrier delivery van. The paramedics that made the scene actually touched Blue this time to verify his was dead. They did so mainly because the cop at the scene named Bubba Warner demanded they do so. The third time was the charm, however, and Blue Steele stayed dead from then on.

The morning Blue died he'd been headed to a corner store in search of his wake-up medicine. That was when he was run over. He'd made it to the middle of the street when he got kissed by a front bumper and fell into the street. Then he had a Gates tire run over his midsection. His daily wake-up medicine consisted of a 40-ounce bottle of malt liquor for the shakes and a BC powder for his daily morning hangover. A local ambulance-chasing lawyer paid for a cut rate funeral for Ol' Blue. He figured he could make a few bucks in a quick settlement and the family was too stupid to know otherwise. The oddest thing about the late Mister Steele's death, though, was discovered at the funeral home. After he had been scrubbed down and deloused, Blue was discovered to have white hair. His wake was the first that anyone in his family knew he wasn't still black-headed.

This story has been brought to you from the land of recessive genes—where family trees do not fork often enough and heifer calves are always nervous. Nowhere else but eastern Texas.

FIFTY-FOUR

······································

TWINKLE TOES

Marvin Celestine was an up-and-coming young thug in a less-than-scenic sector of southeast Houston (if there is a scenic part to be found in the area). He was well on his way to infamy or criminality when a twist of fate and a flare for fashion made him a laughing stock within his peer group. He hung out in all of the right places and associated with the correct lower forms of life to make himself one of *Da Boyz*. Marvin, however, had taken to wearing some tennis shoes that had LED lights incorporated into their soles. These flashing twinkle lights wrapped themselves completely around the whole of the heel area of his footwear. The lights flashed every time he took a step and he thought them ever so stylish. His choice as to how he was shod ultimately was his undoing in his peer group within the street "Gangsta" community.

It was about three thirty on a Saturday morning when an incident occurred that would mark him for life.

The nightclubs had closed and the street trash such as himself were seeking rocks to crawl up underneath before the sun came up. Marvin was driving a stolen (naturally) Lexus and was headed toward a combat zone apartment complex dubbed The Village by the area residents. Within that complex lived a lady that he wanted to lay up with for the night. He had a couple of crack rocks with him and knew she would greet him with both open arms and thighs because of the dope he brought. He told his buddies he was taking a "piece offering" with him.

Celestine and other gentlemen of his class do not live anywhere, but simply live around as free agents. HUD Section 8 housing gives the Baby Mommas a place to live (stay) and the traveling stud ducks drift in and out of their abodes and bedrooms all day and night. These men (if you can call them that) live off of the women with a spoiled child mentality rather than choosing to support themselves. The indiscriminate breeding habits of this population lend themselves to a self-perpetuating genetic cess pool status.

The apartment complex Marvin was headed for was (and still is) located at the dead end of Martin Luther King Blvd. just a couple of miles south of the 610 Loop. He made it as far as Bellfort Street when a couple of night shift cops tried to pull him over because of a burned-out left rear tail light. The chase was on with

Loverboy running west through the subdivisions that he had grown up in. He hit a curb and blew a tire about three minutes into the chase, but not before a police helicopter had gotten overhead. Celestine hit the ground running and took off through yards and over fences. He was making far better time than the cops who were chasing him. Marvin was not weighed down with a gun belt or a bullet proof vest and he had a vested interest in his own freedom. As such he was pulling away from the cops in the foot race. His undoing, however, was his fashion statement sneakers. The overhead helicopter was able to lead ground units to his ever-changing position because his shoes lit up with every step he took. He was boxed in and tackled before he knew it. Then somehow the fleet-of-foot fashion plate slipped and fell down several times along the way as the blue suits walked him back to their patrol car.

He was also dubbed Twinkle Toes by the cops that night, and the nickname stuck. Instructors at the police academy always told each class of cadets the story. He became famous after that night. It is socially acceptable to be an auto thief in Houston (Harris County), Texas nowadays, so Marvin did not spend but half a year of his life in detention for this escapade. However all of the training officers after his release would make a point of stopping him on the street and introducing Twinkle Toes to their rookies. The rookies would often laugh out loud and tell Marvin that they had heard of him in the police academy. He was famous, because the cops were only too willing to tell how he lit up his own path all the way to the jailhouse. Marvin did not stay in Sunnyside for more than eighteen months after his parole before he drifted off. It is hard to be taken seriously as a neighborhood bad-ass when everyone from the cops to other pieces of street trash call you Twinkle Toes all the time.

FIFTY-FIVE

....

WINEAUX CASES

There is a subculture in our society of people who live on the streets. Their population is predominantly male and Anglo. They have their own culture and a vocabulary of sorts. These folks are generally homeless by choice, and live on the street through hustling and through handouts from charity organizations. They live in shelters and missions sometimes, but many chose to live under bridges or in shanty houses that they construct out of cardboard and discarded building materials. The shacks or shelters they build may be under bridges or in wooded area or vacant lots. Their pathetic lives exist in an extremely harsh world. These people defend the shanties they live in (sometimes called camps) very fiercely. There is still a lot of undeveloped land in close proximity to downtown Houston and along the bayous that merge with the Houston Ship Channel. One of the largest colonies of these shacks is under the major street bridge that goes over Buffalo Bayou in the downtown

portion of Houston. There are shacks built directly under the bridges in question. Some of the inhabitants are
industrious enough to tap into electrical lines that run in
the area for free utilities. There again, sometimes they
mess up and electrocute themselves as they are pirating
power. It is a savage and filthy world they live in and the
people therein are invisible to polite society for the most
part.

When a wino or street person becomes a witness in
one of your murder cases you learn how to get his personal information. Important questions are ones like:
What names are you known by on the street? Where to
you stay in the winter months, or the summer months?
Who can I leave word with when I need to reach you in
the future? Do you work at a day labor pool? Criminal
trials often take six months before they come up on
some district court dockets, and your street person is a
free agent. When trial time comes up you may have to
run him past the Salvation Army for a bath and fresh
clothes so you can stand being in the courtroom with
him for testimony. You may also have to get him a beer
during the court's lunch break to ward off the shakes.

Assaults, cuttings and homicides are very common in
the world of the street people. The motivation behind
their murders may be something as minor as "disre-
specting" someone's camp, or at times fighting over
food. One gentleman of the street killed another over a

freshly-killed possum they both savored for an evening meal. Both the DRT (dead right there) wino and the possum appeared in the crime scene photos. Another fatal stabbing occurred because two street scholars argued over whether one of them had more beans on his plate than the other. Life is often very cheap. Street cops always expect a street person will be carrying a weapon. When a wino gets a bottle he expects to get drunk and pass out or go to sleep. He will take his knife and open it and put it in his front pants pocket point up so that if someone tries to go through his pockets while he is passed out they will cut themselves. Street cops don't like dealing with passed out or sleeping "Jakes" for that reason. They may also wake up mean and fighting, or have open knives or needles in their pockets when you go to searching them for weapon. Disease is rampant in this population and as a whole, the population is unclean.

Many of the individuals in question could be described as bordering on mental illness, but they are not stupid. If they were they would not survive. Some of these folks are on Social Security disability and some on pensions from their military service. One of the oddest things about them is that many get their pension checks sent to them at a city or county jail because that is the only permanent address they can claim. Further, a large portion of this population has chemical dependency problems with regard to alcohol or drugs. Many, if not most, of the assaults, stabbings and murders take place when either one or the other of the involved parties involved is under the influence of an intoxicant.

The following confession was taken from a drunken ex-con street person who had just stabbed another Roads Scholar (not Rhodes Scholar) to death. The investigator that took his statement would later testify that yes, in fact, the man had obviously been drinking prior to his giving the confession, but he did not appear intoxicated when he gave or signed the statement. The killer could not read or write. Therefore by law his confession had to be read to him by two non-sworn civilians prior to his signing or it. Two clerks from Homicide's front desk were pressed into service. They read the statement to the suspect and witnessed its signing. The suspect was basking in his wine-induced glory when he gave his statement and all the while it was being read out loud to him by the two partridge-shaped women. He signed it gladly with much bravado.

Stone-cold sober and in a courtroom, the statement did not sound nearly as good when it was read into the record. When it came trail time the defendant refused to plead guilty to a twenty-year sentence. He declared "I ain't taking nothing—you're gonna have to give it to me." Due to his extensive criminal background, a jury awarded the defendant thirty-five years to ponder upon his crime. In fact he had almost certainly been given a life sentence due to his age. See the suspect's confession that follows.

Statement of Person in Custody

State of Texas   County of Harris
June 19th 200X   Time: 7:30 PM

Prior to the making of this statement I, Russell Gallier, have been warned by Sergeant Paul Johnson that:

1. I have the right to remain silent while in custody and not make any statement at all, and any statement that I make may be used against me at my trial.
2. I have the right to have an attorney present to advise me during any questioning by police or lawyers representing the state. If I cannot afford a lawyer one will be appointed to me without charge.
3. I have the right to terminate this interview at any time.
4. Prior to, and during the making of, this statement I do waive these rights and make this statement of my own free will.

I am in Houston PD's Homicide Division because I stabbed Willie Myers earlier tonight. He had it coming. He was a worthless piece of shit, smart-mouthed punk and I'd just had enough of his stuff. He walked up to me while I was standing outside the Star of Hope Mission. I was smoking a cigarette I had just rolled and he slapped it out of my hand. He told me "Old man, get out of my way—you stink." That was all I needed to go off on him.

He was as sorry as an egg-sucking dog and lower than a rattlesnake. I stabbed him first in the back and then a couple of times in the belly when he turned around. I am not afraid of jail and can do my time gladly. F**k the Judge, F**k Huntsville. I'll do my time, and I will say that it really was worth it.

_____

Signature of Person Making Statement

_____

Witness

_____

Witness

FIFTY-SIX

....

YOU TELL ME

Michael Herschel was a normal enough guy through high school and up until he was about nineteen. After that, it was as if a switch was thrown in his head and everything went out of kilter. Almost overnight he became very reclusive and paranoid. At one point he even became violent toward family members. He was put into the Harris County Psychiatric Hospital a time or two for stretches up to ten days. Medication made him manageable and he lived at home with his parents. The good doctors at the "Nut Hut" said he would be functional in a family setting for the most part—but that the frustration of a workplace setting would be more than he could bear up under. Mom and Dad were told to make sure he got his medication daily and to stress him as little as possible. Mike went on Social Security disability (known as SSI) to defray the costs of housing and caring for him.

Our case study had been out of high school for five years when he murdered an elderly husband and wife who lived two doors down the street from his parent's home. A witness living across the street from the murder scene saw Mike exiting the victim's home with what appeared to be blood all over his shirt front. The bodies were discovered along with a bloody ball peen hammer that would later yield two fingerprints of the suspect Herschel. A bloody hand print was also found inside the front door. When it was sprayed with the right chemicals it yielded Mike's fingerprints that were able to be photographed and identified positively.

The suspect was arrested and hustled off to the central police station for an interview and possible confession. A detective named Martin Jackson was picked by the duty lieutenant to interview the suspect. That particular lieutenant was a supervisor that wanted to be highly involved in every case and everything his troops did. He instructed the detective what he wanted him to cover in the interview and specifically to ask the suspect about what medications he was taking for his mental problems and what, if any, effect those drugs had on him.

The killer was interviewed by Marty Jackson and he readily admitted bludgeoning the elderly couple. He gave explicit details as to just how he accomplished his crime. The odd part is that he claimed he had been directed to kill them by his former high school football coach.

Hershel told the detective that he had no choice in the matter because the attack was in the coach's play book. "If you don't do what's in the coach's playbook you'll get kicked off the football team, you know."

Martin Jackson made sure he covered all of the details that his anal-retentive lieutenant wanted included or touched on during the interview/confession. He asked what drugs the suspect was prescribed and if he used any recreational drugs in conjunction with them. Hershel knew the name of the drugs and the dosage that he took. He also advised the investigator that he had taken his medications on the day in question and that he never took illegal drugs. Jackson then asked the fruit-cake/suspect if the drugs he was taking had been doing him any good. The answer came back in the matter-of-fact response "You tell me Detective. I just killed two people this afternoon."

FIFTY-SEVEN

···

HOW DO YOU COPE?

Having to shoot someone affects every officer differently. Some stay angry for an extended time with the person they were forced to shoot or kill. Others are able to simply push it out of their mind. An officer who was forced to kill a sixteen-year-old that pointed a pistol at him told me that he chose not to ever think of it again after that night and he did not. This was a man who was into martial arts where the control of self was of major importance to him. The macho side of policemen often pushes them to face their fear. This is done to show the suspect they faced (be he living or dead) that they are not in control. For all their bravado, the act of having to kill someone puts a mark on officers, some more than others. Post-Traumatic Stress Disorder exists and does occur. One officer who had killed several men during wartime was put into a seriously depressed state following a shootout where he and his partner killed an armed burglar. Just because it did not bother you in the past does not mean PTSD can't strike you in the future. Now, with the politically correct side of life, officers often fear for their jobs if the city or county they work for gets pressured by poverty pimps seeking TV and radio time. I have only known two officers to sue over false allegations made when someone was trying to make news. The first was a black newspaper that alleged two officers committed a murder. The second was a white drug attorney another officer sued who alleged that officer was guilty of murdering his wealthy degenerate drug-using client.

Officer Ismael (Mike) Noonez came under fire when he pulled up on a holdup alarm at a large bank at the intersection of the Gulf Freeway and Almeda-Genoa Road. The suspect was shooting a .30-caliber handgun called an Enforcer at the cops. It looked like a cut down military M1 carbine with a pistol grip and a 12-inch long barrel. A second police car pulled up and blocked the drive at the freeway service road. The second patrol car also drew fire and the officer inside it was wounded in the leg. The bank robber had a female hostage so the officers did not return fire for fear of injuring the innocent bank teller.

The suspect kept both officers pinned down until yet a third blue suit came up behind him and shot the hemmed-in jacker in the back of the head. Ismael was not injured in the incident but he was madder than hell.

Mike Noonez, for several months after the incident, would park his patrol car in the same spot in that bank parking lot every day and eat his lunch. The location he always chose was the same one he had been when pinned down by the bank robber. Every day, as soon as Noonez pulled up he would get out of his car and go to a live oak tree to look at a bullet strike about 6'2" above ground level. If Mike had been three to four inches taller he would have been hit in the forehead by the bullet he'd heard rip over his head. This daily ritual was his way of thumbing his nose at the man who tried to kill him.

Shelby Lewis rode the evening shift out of the Central Station, coming to work daily at three in the afternoon. one Saturday evening he responded to a 911 hang-up call at XXXX East 7½ Street. An alcoholic ex-con named John Harris had just finished beating his wife again, but this time he got carried away. Doris Harris was beaten bloody and was unconscious. Lewis had two years on the department at this point in his career. The front door was ajar as he approached the house and he pushed it open. John Harris was standing over his wife in the kitchen. Lewis could see the blood on the sheet vinyl floor that she laid on. Shelby drew his pistol and approached the suspect. Stupid grabbed up a paring knife off the counter and called out to the young officer, "What ya' gonna do now Bitch—I'm in my own house!"

Shelby had seen a recent training film regarding defending against edged weapons. It taught that if you are within twenty-one feet of a suspect with a knife you are in serious danger. Officer Lewis responded with two 230-grain Hydro-Shock bullets. John Harris was rehabilitated and died at the scene. His wife recovered from the injuries he'd inflicted upon her that night.

Mrs. Harris discovered that her late husband's life insurance would not pay off due to the fact he was in the commission of a felony at the time of his death. After this realization she tried to claim that Saint John was murdered and not armed with a knife. Her lies were disproved one after another. How his bloody fingerprints made with her blood appeared on the knife in question she could not explain.

Twice every year (both on the anniversary of both John Harris' birth and death) Officer Shelby Lewis would go buy a cold six-pack of beer after he got off work. He would finish drinking the beer a little before sundown. Then he would drive to the cemetery where John Harris was buried. Upon arrival there he would urinate upon John Harris' headstone. He did this for five years in a row.

On the sixth anniversary of Harris' death he found that Doris Harris was now also dead and had been buried beside her ex-con wife-beating piece of trash husband. Shelby took the time to piss on both of their headstones. From then on he never repeated this ritual again. He related to me that by that point in history he felt he had adequately expressed his opinion and vindicated himself.

FIFTY-EIGHT

··

HE NEEDED THAT GUN

It was a non-fatal off-duty police officer involved shooting outside a very large country and western nightclub called Boomers. There were two uniformed Houston officers working the club security extra job that was located near the intersection of the East Freeway (Interstate 10) and Uvalde Street. The clientele that frequented this establishment was blue-collar middle income and mostly Anglo. They for the most part worked in the petrochemical industry and made good money. Money they had—class they didn't. The officer that did the shooting was named Roy Walters. The other officer that he was working with that night was a named Steve Acker. The two cops had been standing together by the front door for over an hour when Steve stepped away momentarily to go to the men's room. Things went south from there.

Bobby Carr's wife Lucille left him just days before the shooting. She'd become involved romantically with a

339

Cloverleaf ex-con badass named Gaston Landry. The jilted husband stood two inches over six feet tall and weighed in at two hundred and twenty-five pounds. Gaston was two hundred and sixty pounds of tattooed ugly and two inches shorter than Bobby. Mrs. Landry's son also carried about twenty or so extra pounds of fat on his carcass. The rest of him was a combination of just Pure-D Mean with a large dose of Just Sorrier Than Hell thrown in for good measure. Both men worked in the chemical plants and were beer joint rounders. Bobby wore close-cropped hair and a trimmed mustache. Gaston looked and acted very much like Bluto on the Popeye the Sailor cartoons.

On the night in question, Bobby drove through the parking lot of Boomer's and spotted the man who stole the affections of sweet Lucille, his beloved beer joint beauty queen. He slammed on his brakes and came to a sliding stop when lover boy was about twenty-five feet from the beer joint's front door. Gaston puffed up like a fighting rooster making ready for a cockfight. With much bravado Landry pulled off his black snap tab western shirt and threw it to the pavement as he shouted, "If you wanna get it on, let's get it on!"

The club's hulking doorman/bouncer (who went by the name of Dumpy) knew both men and also knew the reason for the brewing storm between them. He stepped inside the club to notify the officers working that night of the impending fight between the two range bulls just outside the club's front door. Bobby Carr had come to this fight equipped with a .45-caliber Colt Commander model pistol. Steve Acker was still powdering his nose when Dumpy and Roy Walters stepped out of the front door. They saw the shirtless Gaston rushing at Bobby Carr. Bobby neatly sidestepped the larger man's charge and slapped the raging Tush Hog behind the ear with his satin nickel-plated .45-caliber handgun.

Now there are only two ways to safely carry a single-action 1911 Colt with a round in the chamber. The first is with the hammer all the way down and the safety off. The second is with the hammer at full cock and the thumb safety on. Bobby chose the latter. The only truly safe way ever invented to carry a single-action semi-auto pistol is simple. You need simply to keep your finger off the trigger until you want it to go off. Bobby had chosen the locked-and-cocked manner to carry his pistol, just like most cops do. Carr's .45, however, had its safety come off in the excitement and Bob chose to put his index finger inside the gun's trigger guard. Gaston hit the pavement when he was hit behind the ear with the gun. As Landry tried to get up, Bobby stepped over him and began pistol whipping him again and again. Every time Bobby would slap the side of Gaston's head he would grip hard on his pistol and depress the trigger—causing it to discharge into the parking lot. He bitch-slapped

Gaston a total of four times and the weapon went off each time.

Roy Walters walked outside the club's front doors to see one man on his hands and knees and another man standing over him hitting him with a pistol. Coupling that with the fact the weapon kept going off each time the man on the ground was struck—you've really got to believe that Bobby Carr had Officer Roy Walters's complete and undivided attention. Roy took a defensive position behind a concrete pillar and lined up the front sight of his revolver on the armed man's chest.

Roy got Bobby's attention by calling out, "Hey Asshole." Bobby Carr turned around to face Roy Walton, and as he did so he had his pistol in his hand and pointed it towards the officer. Roy shot Bobby one time in the left chest with a 158-grain jacketed hollow-point bullet fired from a four-inch barreled .357 revolver. The bullet entered but did not exit the armed man's chest cavity. Carr absorbed all the energy that the .357 could muster and did so without showing any reaction at all. He stayed on his feet and then just lowered his pistol to where it was pointed muzzle down and at the pavement. He then looked at the officer with what was described to be a shocked expression on his face. Then he looked back at the pistol he held in his hand, and then back at the officer once more. Carr was reported to then drop his .45 to the pavement and kicked it under a parked car.

The officer that did the shooting would later say that Bobby Carr looked rather embarrassed about the whole thing. It was like Bobby was looking at first at the officer and then the handgun as if he was acknowledging that he had accidentally pointed the gun at Walters, and had not meant to. Bobby Carr then just turned and walked away as if nothing had happened.

Roy Walters, the club's doorman and an off-duty deputy sheriff who was coming out of a nearby restaurant had to chase down and fight with the wounded man in order to handcuff him. Gaston Landry (the man who had just been pistol whipped) got up and put his shirt back on and told the cops he did not want to file any sort of charges. He said it was a private matter. Bobby Carr was transported by ambulance to an area hospital for treatment. He refused to speak with either the Homicide or Internal Affairs investigators that came to see him in the emergency room.

The bar's doorman, James "Dumpy" Evans, knew all of the parties involved in this matter. He had also seen the whole thing from its start to the finish. Dumpy went on to tell the IAD and the Homicide sergeants at the scene that Bobby Carr was a really good guy who "was in love with a bitch he can't stand." He also advised the detectives that he only wished Officer Walters had missed Bobby Carr and had accidentally shot and killed Gaston Landry by mistake. The Homicide sergeant at the scene commented that if Mister Carr was such a sterling character, what was he doing carrying a .45 pistol? Dumpy responded with a rather profound piece of northeast Harris County logic by saying, "Hell Sarg, Bobby needed that pistol. That was one bad son-of-a-bitch he was fighting with."

....

FIFTY-NINE

JUST ONE SECOND, OFFICER

American small town life is supposed to be slow and easy going. However when someone looks at the underbelly of Mayberry they quickly discover the warts and sores like drugs and crime that plague the big cities too. Such was the status of a mid- to small north Texas town located between the Dallas and Fort Worth metroplex and the Red River. Sometimes this part of the world is called Baja, Oklahoma. That city had a resident black population at the time of between one thousand and fifteen hundred individuals. Inside that population there were two up-and-coming young Turks that were vying for the title of top dog in town. Either man (on any given day) could be described as a no-account. The men would enter into almost any sort of venture that would bring them fast money and only if it was not associated with honest work. Both scholars were rumored to be transporting dope into town from south Dallas for local distribution. The gentlemen in question were not, however, street dealers. Had they chosen to join forces they could have built a criminal operation that would have been tough to be reckoned with. Fortunately (for society) both of them wanted to be the Alpha Dog in town. The men in question were named Tyler (Ty) Crebbs and Rudolph (Rudy) Jacks.

At that point in history the township had a black nightclub which for the younger set was *the* place to go and be seen on either Friday or Saturday nights. The joint was called The Shandy. One Friday night, as Ty Crebbs was walking up to the front door of the club, Rudy Jacks literally exploded out of its front doors.

Jacks had a .357 in his hand and he ran up and began pounding Crebbs with it. Tyler was knocked to the ground, and Rudy was on top of him—steadily pistol whipping him. After about four blows to the head Rudy stuck the revolver in Tyler Crebbs' mouth and cocked the handgun's hammer back. Jacks then began cursing his rival, calling him a punk (faggot) bitch and speaking more than just a little rudely about Rudy's mother and her son's relationship with her. After shaming the man adequately enough, Rudy pulled the weapon out of Tyler's mouth and laid it alongside his battered foe's head. Next he fired one round into the asphalt parking lot beside Crebbs' head. There wasn't any doubt in Tyler's mind that he had just been shot. The concussion and muzzle blast from that .357 going off next to his head rattled the fillings in his teeth and caused him to pass water. The gunshot literally powder burned Ty's left ear. Rudy got up while Crebbs was still in shock and kicked him in the head a couple of times before he strolled to his pearl white Olds 98 and drove off. Tyler Crebbs had been attacked, beaten down and shamed on his own turf. He had one of two choices to make—either leave town or retaliate. He chose the second of the two options in order to reclaim his manhood.

The local police department was a fifty-man (and woman) operation if you included all employees from the chief to the dispatchers. Though they were not called directly to the scene, the word as to what occurred and the likelihood of what was coming was reported to the agency in a hurry. As a department, this put them on a high alert, for anyone who knew either of the men knew that a killing was in the works.

J.T. Williams was riding the swing shift (6 p.m. until 2 a.m.) on the night after the assault on Crebbs took place. He signed onto the radio and drifted south into the sector of town that he felt he was most likely to encounter either of the two men. Williams was northbound on Central when he looked across two lanes of traffic and saw Tyler Crebbs standing behind a low row of hedges that ran parallel to the west side of the street. From the curb to a concrete sidewalk was about four feet. The sidewalk was three feet wide and an almost four-foot-high hedge began eighteen inches west of the sidewalk. Officer Williams noted that Crebbs was carrying either a rifle or shotgun and that he had its butt stock to his shoulder and it looked like he was pointing it down at the ground on the other side of the hedge in question.

Williams passed the armed man and made a U-turn in the street, stopping on the west curb so that he had an engine block between himself and the armed man. J.T. drew down on the suspect and called out to him: "Tyler Crebbs—drop your weapon!" Tyler kept the gun pointed at the ground while he looked up and called out, "Oh yeah, Officer. No problem. Just a second." Then Tyler fired one time into the ground and immediately dropped the 16-gauge shotgun he was holding. In one motion, Crebbs both fired and dropped the gun and quickly jerked his hands over his head with his palms toward the officer. He did this because he knew he had just scared the fire out of the officer by shooting that shotgun.

What the young cop had not seen was Rudolph Jacks lying on the ground on the other side of the hedge. Rudy was now dead as a hammer and would soon be as stiff as a carp. What's more, the world was now a better place. One piece of trash was dead and another was getting off the streets and into the jailhouse. Murder charges were filed and Ty Crebbs pled not guilty to them. Both he and the dead man had lengthy criminal histories. The trail was set and the defendant claimed it had been a justifiable homicide.

The dead man had, in fact, attacked Tyler the night before the killing and had put him in fear of his life. Crebbs, however, did not even bother to make a police report but instead chose to settle the matter himself. Besides the murder charge there was a charge filed of a felon being in possession of a firearm. The jury realized that the dead man was no great loss and they found the defendant guilty of murder and of possessing a firearm. He was given five years to do for the murder and ten years on the felon possessing a firearm charge. The final ruling was sort of an urban renewal verdict plus one felony conviction. Society won twice.

The only unfortunate side of the final outcome was that Rudy Jacks' funeral was paid for out of funds provided by the State of Texas. That may well be the biggest crime that was committed in this whole episode. In cases of violent crimes there is a fund provided by the state from the fines or probation fees paid specifically by persons on probation for committing violent crimes. Even bottom-feeders like Rudy Jacks could be classified as victims and up to ten thousand dollars can be applied for to defray expenses like funerals or medical bills.

....

SIXTY

THE ONLY WAY TO DEAL WITH ONE

I came into law enforcement almost three a half decades ago up in north Texas. I had to weigh at least 140 pounds to get on with the city police department I wanted to join. I lived on hamburgers, French fries, along with bananas and milkshakes for a week before my physical. When I went in for my physical, the scales said I weighed in at a whopping 137 pounds. The good doctor lied for me and claimed I came in one pound over the minimum.

First, I took a job with a city police department for a couple of years and then I shifted over to the Sheriff's Department there. Following the next election, a card-carrying idiot was put into office. I knew that I couldn't work for him and I'd been in the area for ten years as a lawman and was well known. People tried to convince me to hang around the area and run against the new sheriff during the next election cycle. I thought I might be able to win because I knew the sheriff-elect would step on his tail in a couple of years and either get run out of town or go to prison.

Anyway, I left the employ of that county as soon as the new High Sheriff was sworn in. I had been offered the job of chief deputy in a rural county down in the Big Bend Country. The new sheriff down there was a retired Texas Ranger and he had been stationed up in the northern part of the state while I was learning my way around law enforcement. Upon taking the job, I quickly fell in love with the mountains and the high desert country. That old man was one of the finest folks I'd ever met and he taught me a lot about policing, dealing with people, and running an agency that was part of a county government system.

Another life lesson the old sheriff taught me was about dealing with truly evil people. In all areas of the world there are some people who are without morals and just no damned good. The really bad ones tend to be darned smart and cagy. You are gonna be hard-pressed to make a case on them, and they will terrorize the good folks in your county. They are not opposed to killing witnesses that point them out and many times these individuals come from a family that acts as a unit. They will attack you or anyone else that gets in their way. These folks also will usually take a whole lot of killing. If you do happen to shoot one of 'em you better reload 'cause you might have to shoot them again. That, and the rest of their clan will likely be coming for you. Most decent people either can't conceive that there are people out there like that, or they just don't want to believe anyone can be that consumed by evil.

Well, the old Ranger-turned-Sheriff imparted one thing to me in dealing with these human predators. He told me, and I quote: "The only way you can make them understand is to catch them off by themselves and just whip them 'til they shit all over themselves. Then and only then will they straighten out or leave the area." I have had the occasion to see that process meted out, and it does in fact work. Don't disfigure the bastard's face, though. If you do, the hate in him will well up every time he looks in the mirror. Then he will look for a chance to back shoot you for the rest of his life. You have to catch him out away from everybody and either kill him or whip him until he shits all over himself.

SIXTY-ONE

....

WEAPON OF MASS
DESTRUCTION

Jose Alvarez was a loud-mouthed north side Houston
"Meskin." He was foul mouthed to the point that a lot
of people and most decent women didn't want to be
around him. Joe was a truck driver and had just driven
out of Louisiana from a hot shot delivery and was headed back to Houston when he stopped for fuel. The gas
station he stopped in was about twenty miles over the
state line into Texas in a city called Beaumont. Joe pulled
his pickup into a truck stop where he filled up with
gasoline, and as he was getting back into the truck cab a
gentleman of the street came up and grabbed him by the
arm and jerked him out of the truck. Now Jose is living
proof regarding the adage about all Mexicans carrying
knives. He carries the biggest lock blade knife that Texas
law will allow, clipped to his right front pants pocket. He
was not afraid to use this serrated piece of cutlery on the
day in question when he laid Cassius Mouton's belly

open. In the process, both men got pretty well covered in blood. Cassius was holding his chitterlings in both hands and howling like a banshee while Joe was screaming and cursing, simply acting like he does every other day of his life.

When the bloody men were noticed by the rest of the truck stop patrons there was a whole lot of, *Oh Lauds* and *Oh Jaysus-ing* going on. One ambulance, one fire truck and five police cars responded. The paramedics had to hose off both Joe and the cutting victim because they just couldn't believe Joe wasn't seriously injured with all the blood he had all over him too. What Alvarez lacked intact he made up for with profanity and volume. It didn't take long for him to alienate himself from the puss-gutted cop with a shaved head and walrus mustache who was running the crime scene. Before it was all over Joe was in handcuffs and Cassius was in an ambulance and one fat cop was still trying to figure out what he had and who he disliked the most in the whole situation. You see, even on one of his best days, Himself could at times have been referred to as a Planned Parenthood poster child.

The skinned headed policeman had a unit go the hospital and see what semblance of truth they might get out of the transient cutting victim and they took the rowdy Hispanic monogram artist to the police station to check him out and get a statement out if him if possible.

They found out that Joe's mother must have been scared by a public address system before he was born because he was louder than hell and he would not shut up. He was put in a holding cell while they checked his criminal history and tried to determine just who and what they were dealing with.

This whole time Alvarez was screaming that he wanted his lawyer and this was America and he was not some Wetback who had to put up with being treated like this. Pus Gut the lawman came in shortly and asked Joe what he had been doing with a Colt .45 pistol and a pump shotgun in his truck. Joe said he had been working in Louisiana and he had a license to carry the pistol. He tried to explain that he had been working in south Louisiana and that he knew he could not get a decent funeral down there so he had carried both weapons for protection. The local lawman then proclaimed, "But that there's a model 37 pump Ithaca shotgun. If you hold the trigger down and pump it, that weapon will slam fire every time the action closes. That makes it a Weapon of Mass Deeestruction." Jose then lost his cool and shouted out: "Well then I guess that makes me Osama Ben Alvarez the terrorist from the north side of Houston, doesn't it, you fat hick? Now have you had the common since to check the security video tapes at the truck stop? They will verify that I was attacked by that stupid bastard after I gassed my truck up. Or have you been too busy being the Big Dog around here to find out who the real victim here is?"

Pus Gut had a unit go and recover the security tapes from the truck stop. The video showed Home Boy stalking Joe and jerking him out of the truck and trying to hit Joe with his balled-up fist. This was just before Cassius was allowed to hold his own tripe in his hands for several minutes. The jail cell was opened and the north side Meskin was released. Joe refused to give a statement after being put in a jail cell and told the cops to kiss his posterior and subpoena him before a grand jury when they decided to indict Homey for *robbery by assault*. They kept his knife and guns as evidence, pending a review of the case by the District Attorney's Office. Cassius was ultimately charged with *robbery by assault* and Joe got his guns back after his lawyer threatened to sue the city of Beaumont.

....

SIXTY-TWO

LISTEN TO MOMMA

John Kopic was raised on the A.P. George Ranch in Fort Bend County, Texas. The ranch is bordered on the east by the Brazos River and is about twenty miles inland from the Gulf of Mexico. John's grandfather was the hardnosed Bohemian foreman of that historic parcel of real estate. Fixing fence, plowing, planting and pulling calves was a way of life for Kopic, as well as his father, uncles and cousins. At age twenty-one and after an exceedingly hot summer, both John and his cousin Roger decided to go into a line of work that wouldn't work them like dogs—so they chose to go into law enforcement. John opted to join the Houston Police Department and Roger chose to the Texas Department of Public Safety. Roger could not fathom big city life and John sought a bigger pay check with the city.

Following the police academy, John was assigned to the Beechnut Station. He rode District 15, a lower socio-economic zone that separated southwest and southeast

Houston. The area include the Astrodome and was south of the Texas Medical Center. Now (as was the case then) Houston attempted to maximize their police exposure by putting only one officer per marked car. By doing so they do in fact have more police units on the street, but the number of resisting arrest cases became higher as did the number of duty-related injuries. Kopic stood 5'10" tall and weighed in at about 150 pounds. He was not the biggest guy in town, so he always chose to keep himself in good physical shape. At this point in time the Houston Police Department had a reputation for brutality.

Texas Monthly magazine had just proclaimed the Houston Police "the new gang in town" and their front page cover showed a cop's back clothed in motorcycle gang colors like those flown by the Bandidos or Hell's Angels. The rockers, however, just read *Houston* and *Police*. The department was very short-handed at this time, and their reputation very likely saved many cops from getting injured as the street trash had seen what the blue suits were capable of doing.

One afternoon, John stopped a Maroon Mercury Marquis on Cullen Boulevard just two blocks south of the 610 Loop. The car had an expired safety inspection sticker and was occupied by two of the biggest people that Kopic had ever seen. They filled the whole front end of the car in question and each weighted an estimated three hundred and fifty pounds. Later that night, John described the duo as looking rather like two bull frogs stuffed into a half-gallon jar. The car's driver was a male between thirty and thirty-five years of age and one hundred of his pounds were judged to be fat. The remainder of his bulk the country boy cop judged was very likely beef. The woman in the passenger seat was about twenty-five years older than the driver, and every bit as large.

John approached the driver's door and advised the huge male seated therein "I need to see your driver's license and proof of insurance." The answer from Sunnyside's version of The Incredible Hulk was a resounding "F*** You!" John decided .to make another run at it and responded "Can you hear me clearly, Sir?"

Gordo grunted an answer of some sort so Kopic continued on with this one-sided conversation (such as it was). "Before this interview goes further downhill, I need to see your driver's license and proof of insurance."

Big Boy repeated his prior greeting of "F*** You!" Right then, the front seat passenger slapped the driver's upper right arm with a resounding crack. John described the slap as sounding like a .22 short had gone off inside the car. Then the lady yelled out, "Ralphie, that's one of them crazy f***ing Houston Laws. Now you give him your damned driver's license and such before he calls a bunch of his friends over here and they stomp a mud hole in your ass."

Ralphie fished out his driver's license, got his citation and was on his way shortly. He didn't like it, but he just did like his Momma told him. He also probably saved himself from just the type of grief the old woman warned him about and a trip to jail. Mommas know these things sometimes.

SIXTY-THREE

....

HECKLE AND JECKLE

Dillon Pastor was a wealthy closet case homosexual that both lived and died in the small town of Superior, Wisconsin. He was a big contributor, fund raiser and supporter of both the local police and fire departments. What the local businessman did not want the hometown folks to know was that he was a great fan of tattooed street punks that he could rent for a few hours or for a few days. Pastor apparently really liked to find wayward trash in the nearby town of Duluth's bus station and keep them for a day or two. Plying the street trash with money, drugs or alcohol, this man paid rent for a day or so of twisted pleasures. His hidden lifestyle proved his undoing one winter night at the hands of two equally worthless pieces of human filth. The pair killed him before they took his car, cash and credits cards. Then the vermin fled to Texas. It was the use of Dillon's credit cards by the nineteen- and twenty-year-old Street

Goths that got them arrested in Houston on the day after the body was found.

When Dillon's first business employee arrived and
failed to find the boss in his office already, it was unheard of. By eight thirty his shop foreman began calling
Pastor's house. At nine that morning said foreman went
to his employer's house and found him naked and dead
on his bedroom floor. Pastor had been beaten and
stabbed to death. His house had been looted, which is
typical in these sorts of cases. The local cops noted very
quickly that the dead man's car and wallet were also
missing in action. A credit check on the late closet-case
businessman showed his credit card information and the
cards showed to still be in use and were tracked all the
way from Wisconsin to Texas. In fact, one of them
showed to have been used early on the day the body was
found. It was used to check into a rather high-dollar hotel on Houston's north side.

The Wisconsin cops called Houston's cops and some
burly detectives knocked on a hotel room door and
jacked up a couple of scruffy no-good Goth-looking
street animals. The suspects were transported to the
downtown police station and both readily gave confessions regarding the killing of a middle-aged well-to-do
fagot back in Wisconsin. The Yankeeland cops and the
hometown folks were elated. Confessions were taken by
the Houston detectives and copies of them were faxed to

the Superior police. The hometown boys filed a warrant for the arrest of two dirt bags who were now housed in the City of Houston jail. No less than the Chief of Police of Superior Wisconsin and a detective flew into Houston to take custody of the two defendants and to recover any and all evidence possible.

The detectives that arrested the suspects were assigned to assist the out-of-town officers. The two were named Haskel and Jenkins, but they had long been known as Heckle and Jeckle by their coworkers and supervisors. The men were so called because their antics resembled those of the cartoon characters. The Scandinavian-looking Yankee cops reviewed the HPD offense report and the suspects' confessions. They re-interviewed both of the suspects, who had been relocated into the Harris County jail. The north country law men were a bit astounded by both the vast size of the city of Houston and the overwhelming summer heat and humidity.

At noon on the first day the men were doing their Texas follow-up investigation, the Yankees mentioned they'd like to try some authentic Mexican food. Haskel had spent his teenage years in Mexico and was more than fluent in Spanish. He took the unwitting strangers to a restaurant where all of the menus were in Spanish and the cops were the only people speaking English.

Because the two unsuspecting policemen were unable to read the menus, they had Haskel order for them. The dishes he ordered were so hot and highly seasoned that Jenkins thought you could likely weld boiler plates with it if you wanted to. The poor Yankees would take a bite of lunch and then take a gulp of iced water, followed by a sip of cold beer. Then they would repeat the process all over again. The poor devils had sweat running down the sides of their faces and fire coming out of their noses. All the while, Haskel was advising them that they were eating the mildest items on the menu and what the local cops were eating was just too hot for the Cops del Norte to handle. The Wisconsin cops remained in Houston for two more days, before they left with their prisoners. For those next two days they lived on Pepto Bismol to try and put the fire out in their guts and keep themselves out of the toilet for as long as possible.

The suspects waived extradition and flew back to cold country with the pink-complexed policemen. Two days after the Wisconsin cops return to Superior, the chief of police suffered a mild heart attack. Haskel said (upon hearing of the man's heart attack) that he almost felt guilty for possibly being a contributor to the cop's brush with death—almost. Three months after the arrest of the two BB-brained suspects, Haskel and Jenkins got to go to Wisconsin for the trial of Saint Dillon Pastor's killers. The whole town could not do enough for them. The cops got to catch huge lake trout on Lake Superior, and they never paid for a meal or a bar tab the whole time they were in town. Crime may not pay (at times) but catching crooks on a few occasions has some perks.

SIXTY-FOUR

....

ZOOT

Zoot Wilkerson was an old time crook. He had a rap sheet two blocks long and his last arrest was for sale of cocaine at the ripe old age of seventy three. The gentleman in question ran a nightclub near the infamous corner of the Lyons and Hill. That intersection for several years running was the most dangerous spot in the city of Houston. For many years more cadavers were found within one hundred yards of that intersection than anywhere else in the city. The only bright spot to that situation was that the dearly departed tended to be lower forms of life and their passing tended to be either OSHA killings or urban blight removal. If you involve yourself in the drug world then death is considered an occupational safety hazard. The nightclub itself was a hell-hole known for its whores, drugs and violence. It seems there was something there for everyone as they say. This fine establishment was legally named and licensed as The Disco Duck. The neighborhood residents, however, called the septic tank The Harbor. The Harbor's name did not signify it was a place of safe refuge. It was so called because the area around the joint sounded like Pearl Harbor under attack every Friday and Saturday night due to all the guns going off so regularly.

The less-than-noble Mister Wilkerson died of a massive heart attack one New Year's Day. He was out on bond for the narcotics sale case at the time of his death. By dying he surely felt he had beaten the system yet one more time. Two weeks before his death, Zoot was stopped by patrol officers as he drove out of a dope haven motel called The Della. He was driving his brand new Lincoln Continental and he was also in the company of a well-known prostitute called Big Titty Marilyn. The officer that stopped the man inquired of him, "Zoot what are you doing out here with a whore? I know at your age you ain't got no more nature, so you couldn't get a hard-on if you wanted to." Zoot answered the cop straight away: "Officer it may not get hard no more, but it still hangs pretty heavy."

There are two things in life that you should never try to do. First you should never try to beat a street animal in a cuss fight. Secondly you must always keep in mind that street trash can out-lie any elected official ever born. Don't even bother ever trying because you'll always be out gunned. This is one of the few constants in life, like the magnetic north pole or the sun rising in the east and setting in the west.

SIXTY-FIVE

···

QUOTES FROM THE UNCOUTH

Warning: These assaults on the English language were committed by professionally crass and/or illiterate individuals. *Do not attempt to use these statements at home.* For a complete appreciation of what has been recorded herein, the reading of these statements aloud may at times be beneficial.

A real criminal is somebody who would mix good whiskey and Coca-Cola. They ought to be horse whipped at the very least.

At my age and from my point of view, if a woman has varicose veins she don't need to wear no mesh stockings.

The number of reasons for a man to get married has declined with the invention of the dishwasher, the clothes washer, and the clothes dryer.

Money may not be able to buy happiness—but it sure as Hell can rent it by the hour.

That ol' boy isn't just a squirrel, he's a squirrel's penis.

An officer describing an ultra-picky lieutenant: *He's the kind of supervisor that will go around trying to pick the fly shit out of pepper.*

Where I live, we've got deed restrictions against people like you even being in our neighborhood.

In this neighborhood one's level of prosperity and wealth is measured or gauged by how many cars you have up on blocks in your front yard.

From a Bubba: *She said I ain't got no couth, can you believe that shit?*

The immortalized words of a well-known and highly-regarded Houston good old boy type surgeon from the University of Texas Health Science Center. These are the words he used (after a couple of cold beers) regarding his opinion on the cosmetic surgery industry in general. *A shit house is still a shit house no matter what color you paint it.*

In contention for the Dumbass of the Year award, several armed robbery suspects were arrested following a neighborhood washateria robbery. One of the suspects inquired of a uniformed policeman: *Do you think we woulda got caught if a bunch uh them people inside that place hadn't a knowed who we was?*

Spoken by a teacher at a Catholic parochial school on the north side of downtown Houston: *The instructors here are either Nuns or state certified school teachers. We are called the lay teachers. We call the Nuns the un-laid teachers.*

An overworked intake clerk in the Homicide Division made the following statement regarding the conversations she had during telephone calls. *I hear it over and over again on the phone—he hit her in the face and either hit or kicked her in the body. Then they always have to add 'and I'm three months' pregnant.' Hell I think black women must stay three months pregnant.*

There was a bar owner named Pete (who owned two barrio beer joints) in San Antonio. He was known to the area police as Saint Pedro, the patron saint of Cerveza.

A statement made by an ex-con owner/operator of several strip joints or totally nude clubs: *I don't care what* the stock market is doing or where interest rates are—there has always been a good market for sin.

An old crime scene unit calling the duty lieutenant regarding his overview of an unknown DOA call: *Well, I guess you might be able to classify it as a natural death—but only because lead is an element found in nature.*

Hell I was thirteen years old before I knew that M-F stood for anything other than a Massey Ferguson tractor. The words of a man raised on a rice farm outside of Eagle Lake, Texas.

Feminist groups were invented so that ugly and/or fat women would have something to do over the weekend. You see, that is about as close to a date as they will ever get. Now they have somebody to compare notes with about the new and the latest in techniques of braiding the hair under their arm pits.

A witness' rendition of the insult that led up to one hell of a fight that culminated in a near-fatal stabbing. *Monique walked up to Tarnisha and tol' her 'You ain't nuttin' but a fifty-cent Ho wid a twenty-five cent discount.' Then they commensed to mother***kin' each other and then they started fightin' like cats. It was B this and H that. Monique got cut under the left titty with a steak knife about thirty to forty seconds into the fight. Then she got to squallin' and carryin' on so that*

Tarnisha just walked off. I kinda expected Tarnisha to mark (cut) her on the face while she was down. I seen her do that sorta thing before you know.

With so many American males now living a free-agent relationship with women (enjoying multiple relationships with no parental responsibilities) there are often confrontations between their multiple women that occur. These are sometimes called *B and H fights* (because that is what they call one another the whole time). There again cops sometimes call these confrontations *Two bitches in heat fighting over a street dog.*

A quote from the manager of a rather exclusive men's club/strip joint regarding his patrons and employees: *The vast majority of these ladies are generally a bunch of drug abusing losers that are either queer for each other or have some Ghetto sewer rat for a boyfriend. I am sure that the diseases they carry would also kick the shit out of penicillin on any given day. If my customer base knew them for what they are they damn sure wouldn't throw hundreds of dollars at them.*

Ben Taub Hospital's emergency room, about midnight. Interview with a drunken beating victim that came in off lower Westheimer Street. He had a split ear, a closed eye and an upper lip that was going to need some stitches. *I ain't really sure just what it was that did this to me.*

It was either a big ugly woman or one of them trans-testicled (transvestite) men in a black leather mini skirt. Hell Officer, I was just being a smartass and all I said was 'Does you mother know you're out Darlin'?' Then all that Kung Foo shit started.

The serial killer Raphael Resendez Ramirez, known as The Railroad Killer, murdered people all over the United States. Shortly after being convicted of capital murder in Texas and being sentenced to death he was identified as the suspect in the murder of a couple in Illinois. A local prosecutor (who may have had political aspirations) wanted to prosecute him. An Illinois state judge, reviewing the warrant information, admonished him in the following manner: We currently have a moratorium on the death penalty here in Illinois. The man in question was convicted in Texas of committing capital murder and he has been sentenced to die for his crimes. They don't have electric chairs down there in Texas anymore—they use electric bleachers.

From the mouth of a man with about thirty-two years in the Homicide Division alone: There are two categories of mourners out there at murder scenes. They are the professional and the amateur. You can spot the amateur quite easily. They always crank up too early and get tired out before the TV cameras arrive. The professional will do nothing until the TV cameras arrive and turn their lights on indicating that they have tape running. The professional will never pass out or swoon *upon a hard surface like asphalt or concrete, and will never fall to the ground near an ant bed.*

From a training officer: I knew that the department had seriously lowered their standards trying to get more warm bodies inside blue uniforms. This point was really driven home for me the first time when I made a burglary scene with a brand new rookie. The house was in a super-rich and high-rolling neighborhood. My trainee walked in and looked around, telling the homeowner, *I can see why they chose to break into your place Mister, you've got some really nice shit in here.*

A statement made by a Central Patrol officer following a rather long foot pursuit of an armed robbery suspect through a low-income neighborhood: *The piece of trash you're chasing just wakes up the German Shepherds in the backyards. That way they are primed and ready to bite you when you get there. You know something else? Clothes lines always seem to be strung throat high for some reason.*

A conversation overheard between two men discussing a restaurant. The older man asked if the food was any good there. The younger man said, *It will do in a pinch.* His mentor snorted and responded, *Hell, so will an eighty-year-old whore but that don't mean it's any good.*

The most prolific auto thief in Texas is named Jack Daniels. He has been credited for the theft of bar patrons' cars multiple times each week in the larger cities in the state. He never damages their cars but simply uses them for the night and then returns them the next morning to the same parking place that he originally stole them from. His method of operations is always the same and he never takes a vacation or so much as a day off. Prophetic words from an old Auto Theft detective.

Following a high-dollar robbery spree that resulted in at least one fatal shooting, the two suspects checked into the Adam's Mark Hotel in Houston's Galleria area. After living high on the hog they got identified and arrested. In the course of their lavish spending they bought cell phones for five hundred dollars apiece. When asked why they were being so extravagant, one of the mental midgets responded: *There you go, thinkin' just like a white man.*

Conversation overheard between a paramedic and driver on a private ambulance in the Cloverleaf section in northeast Harris County. They had just made a gang-related drive-by shooting scene. The wounded party was a mucho macho gang Vato. He refused to be transported to a hospital. The paramedic asked the driver, *Did you see that massive tattoo on that idiot's chest?* The driver responded with, *Yeah, what was it a picture of?* The paramedic replied matter-of-factly, *It was either Jesus or Charles Manson—but I'm really not sure which one it was.*

A southeast Houston patrol unit about midnight responded to a call regarding a suspicious vehicle in a warehouse district at the intersection of Dixie and Mykawa Roads. The officer drove up with his headlights off and located the vehicle in question. He approached the car and shined his flashlight into the car in question—locating a couple in the back seat. The male looked up into the flashlight beam and in a pleading voice said, *Not now Officer—Please, not just now.*

From a tape-recorded interview, where the speaker was a witness to an assault. This was his version of what he saw occur. *Officer I'm telling you just what I saw. Big Junior hit the man sure enough, but he only hit him one time. But when he hit him, it was so hard that I promise you it popped that mother***er's dick string.*

Looking For a Few Good Men
This conversation was overheard between two female civilian employees at the central police station. They were talking about how to find a good man, and what attributes to look for in one.

My Momma is one smart old woman. She tol' me early on—Girl don't you be carrying on with or datin' none of them pointy headed niggas. They's the ones that's always gettin' into trouble. They's the ones you're always gonna be seein' on TV all the time—robbin', stealin', cuttin' and killin'. They's all crazy. Now you take a look at my husband. He gots him a nice round smooth kinda head on him. Listen to me now, that's one of them chief indicators you got to be lookin' for when you're lookin' to find you a really good man.

Emergency Messages

One of the tasks given uniformed officers is to locate far-flung family members and advise them to contact family out of town or out of state when problems arise back home. Officers find out early it is best to not tell folks of the death of a loved one, but instead tell them to call Uncle Harry in Tennessee at a certain phone number. When you work in the Homicide Division, the notification of family members in a case that you are working on may well fall upon you. If an officer from your department has done the killing, the notification will darned sure be done by you or one of your squad and in person. These are the sage words of advice from an old mossy-horned Homicide detective to a youngster he was training: *When you notify a group of people their loved one has passed on, don't ever let anyone touch you. Don't let anyone get between you and the door, and keep your distance from everyone. I can promise that you will be very surprised to find out just how far vomit can spray under the right set of circumstances.*

Poor Grandma

This scene took place in a cemetery. It was a clear, hot and dry-blast furnace kind of central Texas mid-summer day. It was almost noontime. The flag-draped coffin was still above ground and the preacher was coming to the end of his graveside service. He was going through the *Dust to dust, ashes to ashes* routine that everybody and their dog knows was wrapping up the show. The dead man was a decorated military veteran. The immediate family sat upon folding chairs and they had been seated under a canvas awning set up for shade. The dead man's aged sister sat on the front row at the far end. Beside her sat a rather angelic looking little girl about seven to eight years old. The child was holding a purse in her lap and wearing ruffled white socks and black Mary Jane shoes.

At the end of the ceremony a group of men from the local VFW chapter moved forward and gave the 21-gun salute. At this point the old woman became overcome by either the heat, emotion, grief or a combination of all three. She fainted dead away and passed out—slumping onto the ground. For a moment nobody moved and there was complete silence. Then the angelic-looking little girl sitting next to her blurted out, "God Damn— they done shot Grandma!" Uncle Bob sure as hell would have approved and could not have orchestrated it any better himself.

SIXTY-SIX

·····································

A PLAIN-SPOKEN MAN

Breckenridge Porter was a long-time lieutenant in Houston's Homicide Division. He was known for his straightforward approach. Here are two quotes that typified his outlook toward life and the fact that he was as subtle as a brick.

The grandson of a former British Prime Minister was murdered in Houston. His remains had been found in a motel room dead from multiple (twenty-eight) stab wounds. It was determined he had been partying at a gay bar that night and left about 2 a.m. with an unknown person. His car was found to be missing as was his wallet and credit cards. His credit cards were checked and they were being used at the Hilton Hotel at Houston's Intercontinental Airport. Following the street hustler's arrest he gave a complete (though self-serving) confession. A reporter from the British Broadcasting Corporation called for a telephone interview with Breck Porter. *Lieutenant what can you tell me about the murder of the Prime*

Minister's grandson? The answer was a contrite: *From all appearances it would appear to be nothing but a straightforward queer killing.* The journalist was aghast saying, *But Sir, this is the Prime Minister's grandson we are talking about!* His response still remained the same: *I don't care who he was, it's still nothing but an obvious queer killing pure and simple. I can't make it something it's not.*

During his many years in the Homicide Division there was one year with a marked surge in the number of homicides. Reporters hunting a story cornered Breck in the hallway and demanded an answer regarding the upswing in murders. Mr. Porter's answer was straightforward and typical of him. *When I came on this job they were killing each other over dope, money and women. They are still killing each other over dope, money and women. Nothing really changes around here except the locations and the names on the blotter.*

There was only one member of the media that Lt. Porter could not stand. He was a wig-and-blue-sunglasses-wearing television type. That gentleman was habitually late and whenever he would show up demanding an interview, Breckenridge Porter would include the worst profanities he could think of in his statements. By doing so his television interviews would be completely worthless and never make it onto the evening news.

This old war horse of a cop truly loved the Homicide Division and in fact turned down a promotion to Captain because it would mean he would have to transfer out of the division he loved so. The police union building was, in fact, rightfully named for him.

SIXTY-SEVEN

··

UPSET FAMILY

The following is a conversation in the old police station at 61 Riesner Street between a Homicide detective and family members of a murder victim. The suspect had been charged and was out on bond only hours after his arrest. The victim's family was openly hostile towards the police.

I want y'all to listen up 'cause I'm gonna say things about the criminal justice system that nobody will ever tell you. There is nothing I can do that will make you happy about this case. The suspect has the constitutional right to make bond while awaiting trial. I can't bring your loved one back. What's more, if I took the son-of-a-bitch that killed him out back and shot him in the head y'all would complain that he did not suffer enough—and you'd be right. Bad things happen to good people and we have done all we can do to date. To family members that is never enough. I want you to know something else. If you guys continue to act like a bunch of horses asses the district attorney will figure your kid was one too and will not put a lot into prosecuting this case. It is your call from here on out.

The dead man's family calmed down and became pleasant and helpful with everyone involved in the case from then on. The suspect was ultimately convicted and sentenced to twenty years.

SIXTY-EIGHT

THEN Y'ALL SHOWED UP

This quote comes from an investigation at an eastern Texas police shooting scene. The shooting took place in the parking lot of a beer joint (sometimes called a nightclub) at 2:45 a.m. on a Sunday morning. After the club closed, many of the patrons of that establishment would hang out visiting, playing car sound systems too loud, and generally acting like the street vermin they were. One of the brain children in question began screaming and yelling and shooting a pistol in the air. An officer in the area heard the shots. He pulled up and confronted the suspect, who was later identified as a local resident named Dewey Shepherd. The armed man's last mistake on earth was to point his .25 automatic mouse gun at a police officer.

We was all just hangin' out after the club closed. Dewey was pretty well drunked up and actin' the fool. I'm here to tell you, Officer, that sometimes when that boy gets to drinkin' he gets to actin' crazier than a shit house rat. After a little bit of stumbling around and talking stuff, I seen him get his little silver looking gun out of his car. He sometimes will shoot that gun in the air while he is celebratin'. I seen him walking through the parking lot and he would shoot it into the air every now and then. It was going POP--POP--POP. Then y'all (the police) showed up and things went to shit real quick. I heard a real loud BLAM—BLAM—BLAM—BLAM and then everybody started running and screaming. That's all I know about the deal that happened out there tonight.

SIXTY-NINE

....

MY NEW PARTNER

I met the man who was going to be assigned as my
regular partner the day I first reported to Homicide. I
checked in with the evening shift duty lieutenant and he
told me where my desk and overhead were and then he
issued me the keys to my desk. I walked into the back
offices and Alfred T. was sitting there, interrogating a
homosexual murder suspect. The interview with a pris-
oner/suspect of this sort was typical. Homosexual suspects, for some reason, often want to give you their life
story, which often includes who brought them into their
now chosen lifestyle. They also want to talk about the
illegal things that their victim or employer is or was involved in. Then they may get down to finally talking
about the crime you are interested in dealing with.

The flaming sweetheart in this case started going into
his social calendar and lifestyle and Alfred cut him off
immediately. I knew I was going to like this crusty old
bastard when he told Tinker Belle: "I don't give a shit

393

what you had for breakfast this morning, just tell me about the part where you killed the other mother***er." Queeny then shifted gears and told the old detective how the dearly departed got folded, spindled and mutilated. It was all put down on paper in the form of a confession, signed, witnessed and put into the case file. The prisoner was returned to his jail cell where he probably met some nice guy and they all lived happily ever after.

This man and I were regular partners for five and a half years. He taught me a lot about homicide investigation, as well as how to belch, scratch, fart in public and spit tobacco juice into garbage cans.

SEVENTY

....

I WANTED TO KILL HIM

I have always contended that you really have to draw on your professionalism the most when you are dealing with child molesters or suspects that kill children or old people. The toughest time I had keeping my hands off a suspect, however, was in a case where a country clod killed his wife. It wasn't the killing part that got to me though. This brain child had just built himself a fancy new outhouse. He'd dug a six-foot-deep hole with a backhoe and built a two-holer outhouse on top of it. The day after it was finished being built our hero gets pissed at the old lady while the kids are off at school. He proceeds to pick up a hammer and kill her. Then he dismembers the body and puts her remains in the bottom of the outhouse. Then Country Boy pours fifty pounds of lime on top of the body. What made me want to beat him to death, though, was that it took him five full months to develop a conscience. Up until it got to bothering him, he and his three kids had been steadily using that outhouse day in and day out.

His passing judgment over the bitch's remains for almost half a year in the manner he chose to was quite a statement in itself. You could easily laugh at the irony of the whole situation and could find it to be pretty funny. That is, unless you were the one who had to recover the victim's body. Then you might have serious thoughts of becoming an axe murderer yourself.

....

SEVENTY-ONE

WHAT DO YOU WANT TO BE?

In the great state of Texas the penal code contains what is known as the *law of parties*. Basically if you are involved in any part of a criminal episode, then you are guilty of whatever crime any or all of your cohorts have just committed. An example of this might be if you are the driver of a getaway car during a bank robbery you are guilty of aggravated robbery. If someone is killed in the course of that robbery, then you too are also guilty of the capital murder and are eligible for the death penalty. It does not matter that you did not enter the building, make a demand or even handle a gun—you are still a capital murder suspect. There are no conspirators before or after the fact in Texas—simply suspects.

There are times you have a shooter and a lesser-involved party in custody. You need to flip that second person to shore up your case. He might be a getaway driver, or somebody who just happened to be with your shooter. He may have later hidden the murder weapon for the killer. If you don't have much of a case on your shooter, sometimes it doesn't hurt to convince a lesser involved party to become a witness instead of being filed on as a suspect. He will have to testify, and you want to lock him into his statement before a grand jury so he doesn't roll over on you later.

The story will go that you are a witness and were unwittingly drawn into this case. The shooter did not plan with you or tell you that he was going to rob Abdul at the corner grocery. He just asked you for a ride to the corner store and told you to wait on him. When he got back into the car he told you he had just shot somebody during a robbery. That was the first you heard of any armed robbery. Sometimes when you have a cooperative witness and you find something like a prohibited weapon, you may simply confiscate it and you don't file any charges.

You have to find the leverage point that gets this witness you want to come over to your side. To get a reluctant witness off the dime and join the team may take several approaches. Here are a couple of phrases used to get points across. The first and the last of the below paragraphs are universal and very often used. Only one of the middle two paragraphs are generally used. You can pick out which one of the statements that applies and plug it in. Sometimes one or more of these phrases may be applicable.

You seem like a decent enough old boy, and it looks like you just fell in with some bad company. You are in an interesting position. I want you to listen carefully because you've got to make a very important choice tonight. You can be a witness or you can be a suspect. Suspects get high bonds and stay in the county jail for six months before their case comes up for trial. Witnesses go home tonight, but crooks don't. Which group do you want to belong to?

You aren't very big, and you're not gonna do well in jail. They're gonna love it when you get transferred to the joint. You've got just enough spirit in you to squirm pretty good while they punk you on a regular basis. Boy, they're gonna break you open like an old-time shotgun and load you on a regular basis. When you fart nothing is gonna happen but a little puffing sound.

While you're sitting in jail somebody else is gonna be getting all of your pussy, and you're gonna have to learn how to sleep on your back. There's no sweet thing for you to cuddle up to within the night. It's your call. Now where do you want to lay your head for the next fifteen to twenty years?

Now what do you want to be when you go to court— a suspect or a witness?

SEVENTY-TWO

HOW MANY KINDS OF A....

A patrol unit rolled up on a family disturbance as they cruised through the parking lot of the La Chat Nightclub. A wife and her husband had just been ejected from the building for getting into a pushing, shoving and screaming contest inside the business. The loving couple was separated and the wife was the first one allowed to speak her piece. This evaluation gives the cops time to see what they have and who (if anybody) needs to go to jail. Sometimes just letting the parties vent their anger is enough and then you can send everybody on their separate ways.

Officer I've just had enough of his shit. He don't work, and he don't come home at least half the time. Tonight while I was on the dance floor he got into my purse and stole a pint bottle of wine! That's what this whole mess is behind.

The husband had just been standing quietly and listening to his beloved carry on. His response was, *Officer, will you please tell me this—just how many kinds of a mother***er can one man be?*

The cop responded with, Mister, I'm not really sure about that. I'm gonna have to work on that one for a minute.

ABOUT THE AUTHOR

Sgt. Brian Foster retired from the Houston Police Department after thirty-four years of service. Twenty-three of those years were spent in the Houston PD Homicide Division where Foster averaged twenty-five to thirty-eight murder scenes each year.

Foster is now enjoying his retirement in his home state of Texas, along with his wife and dogs, where he is at work on his next book.

Made in the USA
Charleston, SC
28 January 2017